Type 2 Diabetes
30 Minutes Fast Recipe with
Suitable for Beginners

Let diabetes no longer hinder our diet

Diabetes Basics

What is Diabetes?

Salads, with their remarkable diversity and healthful benefits, allow for endless creativity. By combining an array of crisp vegetables, savory proteins, and carefully chosen dressings, anyone can enjoy a nutritious and delectable meal. Salad-making, though brimming with creative potential, remains accessible to all, requiring only basic culinary skills and a love for fresh ingredients to produce visually stunning and palate-pleasing dishes.

Types of Diabetes

Type 1 Diabetes

- Type 1 diabetes is referred to as juvenile-onset diabetes (JOD) and is often called insulin-dependent diabetes (IDD). Usually, it occurs in children or young adults.

Type 2 Diabetes

- Type 2 diabetes is referred to as adult-onset diabetes (AOD) and is often called non-insulin-dependent diabetes (NIDD). It usually occurs later in life and may be linked to obesity or genetics.
- A person with IDD must take insulin tablets daily for life. A person with NIDD must take pills that have a different type of insulin daily for life. Both types are equally likely to develop complications of poorly controlled blood glucose levels such as blindness, kidney failure, and nerve damage (neuropathy).

Symptoms

IDD Symptoms

- Frequent thirst
- Frequent urination
- Unexplained weight loss
- Irritability or unusual tiredness
- Swelling in the feet (peripheral neuropathy)

NIDD Symptoms

- Blurred vision
- Fatigue or weakness
- Blurred speech
- Numbness or tingling sensation in the feet or hands (peripheral neuropathy)
- Excessive weight gain despite a low caloric intake (polyuria)
- Occasional severe leg cramps (painful diabetic nephropathy)
- Muscle wasting (cataracts)
- Mouth sores or other infections

Causes and Prevention

There are many various causes of diabetes, but most cases are caused by lifestyle choices that can be changed. Diabetes is not contagious; it can't be passed from person to person. The only way you can get diabetes is if your body makes it too difficult to use insulin properly. This difficulty is caused by a decrease in a hormone called insulin. Insulin is needed for the body to pull glucose out of the bloodstream (blood sugar) into cells to use as energy. When this happens, glucose starts to build up in the blood because it needs a place to go for strength.

How to Prevent Diabetes

Being aware that someone has diabetes will help you be more aware of their diet, exercise, and blood sugar management. You can help someone with diabetes by talking about good nutrition and taking things slowly when helping them with changes to their diet or exercise regime. You can also store food in various areas of your home when several people might want snacks. Make snacks available in large quantities so that they are easy to munch on without feeling guilty!

Nutrition for People with Diabetes

One of the most essential nutritional guidelines for people with diabetes is understanding carbohydrates. Carbohydrates are easily converted into glucose so that the pancreas can make insulin. The main carbohydrate is called "sugars," which includes table sugars such as white sugar, brown sugars such as brown sugar, and high fructose corn syrup. Avoid foods made with white sugar (also known as "hard" or "raw" sugar), which has approximately 44 grams per 100 grams of calories, meaning it has nearly twice as many calories per gram as refined white sugars!

Common Symptoms of Diabetes

- Weight loss
- Hair loss or changes in hair texture
- Unexplained fatigue
- Unexplained thirst
- Unexplained hunger

Type 1 diabetes is a severe illness and can cause sufferers to go blind or even lose their lives if left untreated long enough. Type 2 diabetes can lead to many complications as well, such as kidney disease and heart disease. Gestational diabetes, or "pregnancy-induced diabetes," often occurs in women who have just given birth. If left untreated, these women will have complications later in life, such as blindness or even death from the complications of diabetes. Luckily, there are ways to avoid these complications by educating yourself about this disease and taking your doctor's advice regarding treatment options.

Tips for Managing Diabetes

- Get your yearly medical checkup often, including a blood test, and don't miss it.
- Eat a balanced diet that will help improve your metabolism without any adverse effects.

About This Cookbook

This cookbook is intended for people who have recently been diagnosed with diabetes and are just beginning to learn about cooking. It's a great way to start enjoying the process of preparing food while learning about diabetes. This cookbook will help you navigate your way through all kinds of food and teach you how

Table of Contents

Table of Contents

Introduction

A diagnosis of diabetes can be frightening. You may be in a state of shock, barely comprehending your doctor's explanations about blood sugar numbers, blood testing, medications, and potential complications. For many, thoughts immediately turn to food. After all, eating is one of life's greatest pleasures. As a certified diabetes educator, the first questions my patients usually ask are, "What can I eat? Will I have to cut out my favorite foods? Are bread, pasta, and sweets off-limits forever? How will I cook for my family if I have to be on a special diet?"

The changes you have to make might feel overwhelming. Conflicting advice from friends and the media can make things even more confusing. But here's the good news: Type 2 diabetes is manageable. Best of all, you will still be able to eat your favorite foods. And yes, that does include bread, pasta, and sweets—in moderation, of course! The Type 2 Diabetic Cookbook and Action Plan is here to help you. We will give you step-by-step guidance on tackling the diet and lifestyle changes that can help you manage type 2 diabetes. So... take a deep breath and read on.

The main goal of type 2 diabetes treatment is to effectively manage your blood sugar through food choices and physical activity. Good blood sugar control is important to help prevent complications. While some people may need medications, the good news is that many can manage their diabetes with lifestyle changes alone. This includes losing weight if you are overweight, exercising regularly, and eating a healthy diet.

In the past, diabetic diets were very restrictive. Thirty years ago, when I first started counseling patients with diabetes, I advised them to avoid sugar and all desserts and to follow a rigid "exchange" type plan. Food was divided into six different groups, or exchange lists, with each list containing foods with about the same amount of carbohydrate, protein, fat, and calories. For example, for breakfast you might be allowed one fruit exchange, two bread exchanges, one milk exchange, one meat exchange, and one fat exchange. While this system can be helpful for meal planning, it can also be somewhat inflexible.

But times have changed! While you will probably need to make some changes in what you are eating, you will have the flexibility to include the foods you enjoy. Adjusting to a new relationship with food can be challenging, and we're here for you every step of the way. We want to make it easy, so you don't feel overwhelmed. That's why we've taken the guesswork out of what to eat to manage your diabetes.

Here is what you will find in this book as we guide you through the first three months:

- Month 1: Learn the basics of a healthy diet and how foods affect your blood sugar and overall health. Get the lowdown on carbohydrate counting and the glycemic index/load. Best of all, use the very clear·instructions for two weeks of meal plans— including detailed shopping lists.

- **Month 2:** Focus on physical activity and stress management, as they play key roles in blood sugar management. Get more details on nutrition, mindful eating, and weight-loss tips. Stock your kitchen and get ready to prepare diabetes-friendly meals.
- **Month 3:** Get practical tips for dealing with diabetes mentally and emotionally. The tips include guidance for social situations, dining out, and troubling moments, as well as other support.

When you have type 2 diabetes, you become a member of a team. Your doctor, nurse, dietitian, certified diabetes educator, pharmacist, psychologist, podiatrist, and other specialists are all working to help you. It's important that you discuss with your team your treatment goals and how to achieve them. Diabetes is not a one-size-fits-all condition, and you need a care plan tailored for you.

Diabetes is not a doomsday diagnosis. On the contrary, I've had many patients tell me that getting diagnosed helped them take better care of themselves. They've lost weight and feel more energetic and healthier overall. Play an active role in your own health and take charge of your diabetes!

Chapter 1:

BREAKFAST

Quinoa Breakfast Cereal

🕐 Preparation Time: 5 minutes
Cook Time: 20 minutes

🍴 Servings: 4

🥗 NUTRITION

Calories	259	Total Carbohydrates	39g
Total Fat	7g	Sugar	10g
Cholesterol	1mg	Fiber	4g
Sodium	38mg	Protein	10g

INGREDIENTS

1 cup water
1 cup skim milk
1 cup uncooked quinoa, thoroughly rinsed
1/2 teaspoon ground cinnamon
Pinch of sea salt
2 tablespoons granulated sweetener
1 teaspoon pure vanilla extract
1/4 cup toasted chopped almonds
1/2cup sliced strawberries

🥣 DIRECTIONS

1. In a medium saucepan over medium-high heat, combine water, milk, quinoa, cinnamon, and salt.
2. Bring the mixture to a boil, then reduce the heat to low.
3. Simmer the quinoa cereal for approximately 15 minutes, until most of the liquid is absorbed.
4. Remove the cereal from heat and stir in the sweetener and vanilla extract.
5. Divide the cereal evenly into four bowls, and top each serving with almonds and strawberries.

Wild Mushroom Frittata

Preparation Time: 5 minutes
Cook Time: 20 minutes

Servings: 4

NUTRITION

Calories -------------------- 226
Total Fat ------------------- 15g
Cholesterol ---------------- 430mg
Sodium ------------------- 223mg
Total Carbohydrates --------- 5g
Sugar ------------------- 4g
Fiber ------------------- 1g
Protein -------------------- 17g

INGREDIENTS

large eggs
/2cup skim milk
/4teaspoon ground nutmeg
ea salt
reshly ground black pepper
teaspoons extra-virgin olive oil
cups sliced wild mushrooms
cremini, oyster, shiitake,
ortobello, etc.)
/2red onion, chopped
teaspoon minced garlic
/2cup goat cheese, crumbled

DIRECTIONS

1. Preheat the broiler.
2. In a medium bowl, whisk together the eggs, milk, and nutmeg until well combined. Season lightly with salt and pepper, then set aside.
3. Place an ovenproof skillet over medium heat and add the olive oil, ensuring the bottom is completely coated by tilting the pan.
4. Saute the mushrooms, onion, and garlic until translucent, approximately 7 minutes.
5. Pour the egg mixture into the skillet and cook until the bottom of the frittata is set, lifting the edges of the cooked egg to allow the uncooked egg to seep under.
6. Place the skillet under the broiler until the top is set, about 1 minute.
7. Sprinkle the crumbled goat cheese over the frittata and broil until the cheese is melted, approximately 1 minute more.
8. Remove from the oven and cut into 4 wedges to serve.

Blueberry Cinnamon Muffins

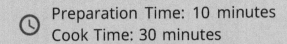

Preparation Time: 10 minutes
Cook Time: 30 minutes

Servings: 10

 NUTRITION

Calories -------------------- 194
Total Carbs -------------------- 12g
Net Carbs -------------------- 10g
Protein -------------------- 5g
Fat -------------------- 14g
Sugar -------------------- 9g
Fiber -------------------- 2g

 DIRECTIONS

1. Preheat the oven to 350 degrees Fahrenheit. Line 10 muffin cups with paper liners.
2. In a large mixing bowl, combine almond flour, Splenda, baking powder, and cinnamon.
3. Stir in eggs, blueberries, half-n-half, and melted margarine. Mix well until fully combined.
4. Fold in the blueberries gently.
5. Spoon the batter evenly into the lined muffin pan.
6. Bake for 25-30 minutes or until a toothpick inserted into the center comes out clean.

 INGREDIENTS

3 eggs
1 cup blueberries
1/3 cup half-n-half
1/4 cup margarine, melted
1 1/2 cup almond flour
1/3 cup Splenda
1 tsp. baking powder
1 tsp. cinnamon

Breakfast Pizza

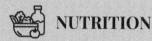

Preparation Time: 10 minutes
Cook Time: 30 minutes

Servings: 10

NUTRITION

Calories -------------------- 230
Total Carbs ------------------- 4g
Protein ------------------ 16g
Fat ------------------ 17g
Sugar ------------------ 2g
Fiber ------------------ 0g

INGREDIENTS

12 eggs
1/2 lb. breakfast sausage
1 cup bell pepper, sliced
1 cup red pepper, sliced
1 cup cheddar cheese, grated
1/2 cup half-n-half
1/2 tsp. salt
1/4 tsp. pepper

DIRECTIONS

1. Preheat the oven to 350 degrees Fahrenheit.
2. In a skillet, brown the breakfast sausage. Transfer to a bowl.
3. Add sliced peppers to the skillet and cook for 3-5 minutes or until they begin to soften. Transfer to a bowl.
4. In a small bowl, whisk together the eggs, half-n-half, salt, and pepper.
5. Pour the egg mixture into the skillet and cook for 5 minutes or until the sides start to set.
6. Bake for 15 minutes.
7. Remove from the oven and set it to broil. Top the "crust" with sausage, peppers, and grated cheddar cheese. Broil until the cheese is melted and starts to brown.
8. Let it rest before slicing and serving.

Simple Buckwheat Porridge

Preparation Time: 5 minutes
Cook Time: 40minutes

Servings: 4

 NUTRITION

Calories	122	Total Carbohydrates	22g
Total Fat	1g	Sugar	4g
Cholesterol	1mg	Fiber	3g
Sodium	48mg	Protein	6g

INGREDIENTS

2 cups raw buckwheat groats
3 cups water
Pinch of sea salt
1 cup unsweetened almond milk

 DIRECTIONS

1. Place the buckwheat groats, water, and salt in a medium saucepan over medium-high heat.
2. Bring the mixture to a boil, then reduce the heat to low.
3. Cook until most of the water is absorbed, about 20 minutes. Stir in the almond milk and cook until very soft, about 15 minutes.
4. Serve the porridge with your favorite toppings such as chopped nuts, sliced banana, or fresh berries.

Cheese Spinach Waffles

 Preparation Time: 10 minutes
Cook Time: 20 minutes

 Servings: 4

NUTRITION

Calories ------------------- 186
Total Carbs ------------------ 2g
Protein ------------------ 14g
Fat ------------------ 14g
Sugar ------------------ 1g
Fiber ------------------ 0g

 ## DIRECTIONS

1. Thaw the spinach and squeeze out as much water as possible, then place it in a large bowl.
2. Preheat your waffle iron and spray with nonstick cooking spray.
3. Add the remaining ingredients to the bowl with the spinach and mix well.
4. Pour small amounts of the mixture onto the waffle iron and cook as you would for regular waffles.
5. Serve warm.

 ## INGREDIENTS

 strips of bacon, cooked and
 rumbled
 eggs, lightly beaten
 /2 cup cauliflower, grated
 /2 cup frozen spinach, chopped
 squeeze water out first)
 /2 cup low-fat mozzarella cheese
 /2 cup low-fat cheddar cheese
 tbsp margarine, melted
 /4 cup reduced-fat Parmesan
 heese, grated
 tsp onion powder
 tsp garlic powder
 Nonstick cooking spray

Spinach and Feta Quiche

DIRECTIONS

1. Preheat the oven to 375°F.
2. Bake the pie shell for about 15 minutes, or until it just begins to turn golden. Remove from the oven and set aside.
3. Heat a large nonstick skillet over medium heat. Spray with cooking spray away from the heat source and return to the heat.
4. Saute the onion until softened, about 5 minutes. Add the garlic and saute for another minute. Add the spinach and roasted pepper, cooking for 1 minute while stirring until heated and the excess water from the spinach is evaporated. Remove from heat and stir in the feta cheese until well combined; set aside.
5. In a large bowl, whisk** together the egg, egg whites, milk, evaporated milk, oregano, and black pepper.
6. Spoon the spinach mixture into the pie shell, spreading it evenly.
7. Ladle the egg mixture over the spinach in the pie shell until it fills the shell, just reaching the inner rim. Depending on the pie shell size, you may have leftover egg mixture, which can be discarded (do not overfill the quiche).
8. Place the quiche on a baking sheet and bake on the middle oven rack for 35 to 40 minutes, or until the quiche is just set. Remove from the oven and let it cool for about 10 minutes. Cut into 8 slices and serve warm.

 Preparation Time: 10 minutes
Cook Time: 80 minutes

 Servings: 8

NUTRITION

Calories -------------------- 192
Fat ------------------- 9.8g
Saturated Fat ------------------ 3.2g
Monounsaturated Fat ------ 3.7g
Polyunsaturated Fat -------- 0.2g
Cholesterol -------------------- 35mg
Sodium -------------------- 321mg
Carbohydrate --------------------
19.9g
Dietary Fiber ------------------- 1.4g
Sugars ------------------- 5.3g
Starches ------------------- 0.5g
Protein ------------------- 8.3g

 INGREDIENTS

1 9-inch frozen reduced-fat pie shell
Canola cooking spray
3/4 cup chopped yellow onion
1 clove garlic, minced
1 10-ounce package frozen chopped spinach, thawed, drained, and excess liquid squeezed out
2 tablespoons chopped roasted red pepper
1/2 cup crumbled feta cheese
1 egg
3 egg whites
1/3 cup fat-free milk
1/2 cup evaporated skim milk
1/4 teaspoon ground dried oregano
Pinch of ground black pepper

Crispy Pita with Canadian Bacon

 Preparation Time: 5 minutes
Cook Time: 15 minutes

Servings: 2

NUTRITION

Calories -------------------- 251
Fat -------------------- 13.9g
Protein -------------------- 13.1g
Carbs ------------------- 20.1g
Fiber ------------------ 3.1g
Sugar ------------------ 0.9g
Sodium ------------------ 400mg

INGREDIENTS

1 (6-inch) whole-grain pita bread
3 teaspoons extra-virgin olive oil, divided
2 eggs
2 Canadian bacon slices
Juice of 1/2 lemon
1 cup microgreens
2 tablespoons crumbled goat cheese
Freshly ground black pepper, to taste

 ## DIRECTIONS

1. Heat a large skillet over medium heat. Cut the pita bread in half and brush each side of both halves with ¼ teaspoon of olive oil (using a total of 1 teaspoon oil). Cook for 2 to 3 minutes on each side, then remove from the skillet.

2. In the same skillet, heat 1 teaspoon of oil over medium heat. Crack the eggs into the skillet and cook until the eggs are set, 2 to 3 minutes. Remove from the skillet.

3. In the same skillet, cook the Canadian bacon for 3 to 5 minutes, flipping once

4. In a large bowl, whisk together the remaining 1 teaspoon of oil and the lemon juice. Add the microgreens and toss to combine.

5. Top each pita half with half of the microgreens, 1 piece of bacon, 1 egg, and 1 tablespoon of goat cheese. Season with pepper and serve.

Coconut and Berry Smoothie

⏱ Preparation Time: 5 minutes
Cook Time: 5 minutes

🍴 Servings: 2

🥗 NUTRITION

Calories -------------------- 182
Total Fat ------------------- 14.9g
Protein ------------------- 5.9g
Carbohydrates ------------ 8.1g

Fiber -------------------- 4.1g
Sugars -------------------- 2.9g
Sodium -------------------- 25mg

INGREDIENTS

1/2 cup mixed berries (blueberries, strawberries, blackberries)
1 tablespoon ground flaxseed
2 tablespoons unsweetened coconut flakes
1/2 cup unsweetened plain coconut milk
1/2 cup leafy greens (kale, spinach)
1/4 cup unsweetened vanilla nonfat yogurt
1/2 cup ice

🥣 DIRECTIONS

1. In a blender jar, combine the mixed berries, ground flaxseed, unsweetened coconut flakes, unsweetened plain coconut milk, leafy greens, unsweetened vanilla nonfat yogurt, and ice.
2. Blend until the mixture is smooth.
3. Pour into glasses and serve immediately.

Creamy Green Smoothie

 Preparation Time: 5 minutes
Cook Time: 5 minutes

 Servings: 2

NUTRITION

Calories -------------------- 172
Total Fat -------------------- 7g
Cholesterol -------------------- 6mg
Sodium -------------------- 110mg
Total Carbohydrates -------------------- 20g
Sugar -------------------- 12g
Fiber -------------------- 4g
Protein -------------------- 8g

DIRECTIONS

1. Put the shredded kale, diced avocado, chopped Granny Smith apple, unsweetened almond milk, plain Greek yogurt, and ice cubes in a blender.
2. Blend until smooth and thick.
3. Pour the smoothie into two glasses and serve immediately.

INGREDIENTS

2 cups shredded kale
1/2 avocado, diced
1/2 Granny Smith apple, unpeeled, cored, and chopped
1 cup unsweetened almond milk
1/4 cup 2 percent plain Greek yogurt
3 ice cubes

Chapter 2:

LUNCH

Cilantro Lime Shrimp

⏰ Preparation Time: 15 minutes
Cook Time: 8 minutes

🍴 Servings: 4

🥗 **NUTRITION**

Calories -------------------- 133
Fat -------------------- 3.5g
Protein -------------------- 24.3g

INGREDIENTS

1/2 teaspoon minced garlic clove
1 pound (454 g) large shrimp, peeled and deveined
1/4 cup chopped fresh cilantro, or more to taste
Zest and juice of 1 lime
1 teaspoon extra virgin olive oil
1/4 teaspoon salt
1/8 teaspoon black pepper

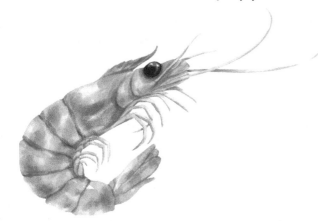

DIRECTIONS

1. In a large heavy skillet, heat the olive oil over medium-high heat.
2. Add the minced garlic and cook for about 30 seconds until fragrant.
3. Toss in the shrimp and cook for approximately 5 to 6 minutes, stirring occasionally, or until they turn pink and opaque.
4. Remove the skillet from the heat and transfer the cooked shrimp to a bowl.
5. Add the chopped cilantro, lime zest, lime juice, salt, and black pepper to the shrimp, and toss gently to combine.
6. Serve the cilantro lime shrimp immediately.

Lemon Parsley White Fish Fillets

| ⏱ Preparation Time: 10 minutes
Cook Time: 10 minutes | 🍴 Servings: 4 |

 **NUTRITION**

Calories -------------------- 283
Fat ------------------- 17.2g
Protein ------------------ 33.3g
Carbs ------------------ 1.0g

Fiber ------------------- 0g
Sugar ------------------- 0g
Sodium ------------------- 74mg

INGREDIENTS

4 (6-ounce / 170-g) lean white fish fillets, rinsed and patted dry
2 tablespoons finely chopped parsley
1/2 teaspoon lemon zest
1/4 teaspoon dried dill
1 medium lemon, halved
Cooking spray
Paprika, to taste
Salt and pepper, to taste
1/4 cup extra virgin olive oil

DIRECTIONS

1. Preheat the oven to 400°F (205°C). Line a baking sheet with aluminum foil and spray with cooking spray.
2. Place the fish fillets on the prepared foil and sprinkle with paprika. Season with salt and pepper according to taste. Bake in the preheated oven for 10 minutes or until the flesh flakes easily with a fork.
3. Meanwhile, in a small bowl, stir together the chopped parsley, lemon zest, olive oil, and dried dill.
4. Remove the fish from the oven and transfer to four plates. Squeeze lemon juice from the halved lemon over the fish.
5. Serve the fish fillets topped with the parsley mixture.

Chicken with Mozzarella Cheese

Preparation Time: 20 minutes
Cook Time: 25 minutes

Servings: 6

NUTRITION

Calories ------------------- 430
Fat ------------------- 19.2g
Sodium ------------------- 320mg
Carbs ------------------ 7.6g
Fiber ------------------ 1.3g
Sugar ------------------ 0.3g
Protein ------------------- 56.8g

INGREDIENTS

tbsp olive oil
/4 cup parmesan cheese, grated
/4 cup smoked mozzarella cheese
tbsp pine nuts, toasted
/4 cup fine dry bread crumbs
/2 10 oz package frozen spinach,
hopped
clove garlic, minced
/4 cup shallots, chopped
alt and pepper to taste
skinless and boneless chicken
reast

DIRECTIONS

1. Place a chicken breast between 2 pieces of plastic wrap.
2. Pound lightly with a meat mallet until it is 1/8 inch thick.
3. Season the chicken with salt and pepper. Repeat the process for all chicken breasts. Set aside.
4. In a medium skillet, cook the garlic and shallots in 2 tablespoon hot oil until they are tender. Remove from the heat and add nuts, spinach and smoked mozzarella.
5. In another bowl, combine the parmesan cheese and bread crumbs. Add to the nut mixture.
6. Place 2 tablespoon of the filling on one side of the chicken breast. Fold the chicken breast then secure with wooden toothpicks.
7. Brush the chicken breasts with olive oil and coat with bread crumbs. Place the chicken seam side down and bake for 400 degrees Fahrenheit for 25 minutes.
8. Remove the toothpicks before serving.

Cajun Catfish

Preparation Time: 5 minutes
Cook Time: 15 minutes

Servings: 4

NUTRITION

Calories	367
Fat	24.0g
Protein	35.2g

DIRECTIONS

1. Heat oven to 450°F (235°C). Spray a baking dish with cooking spray.
2. In a small bowl whisk together everything but catfish. Brush both sides of fillets, using all the spice mix.
3. Bake 10 to 13 minutes or until fish flakes easily with a fork. Serve.

INGREDIENTS

4 (8-ounce / 227-g) catfish fillets

2 teaspoons thyme

1/2teaspoon red hot sauce

2 tablespoons olive oil

2 teaspoons garlic salt

2 teaspoons paprika

1/2teaspoon cayenne pepper

1/4 teaspoon black pepper

Nonstick cooking spray

Lamb and Mushroom Cheese Burgers

🕐 Preparation Time: 15 minutes
Cook Time: 15minutes

🍴 Servings: 4

🥗 **NUTRITION**

Calories -------------------- 172
Fat -------------------- 13.1g
Protein -------------------- 11.1g

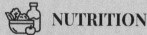 **INGREDIENTS**

8 ounces (227 g) grass-fed ground lamb
8 ounces (227 g) brown mushrooms, finely chopped
1/4 cup crumbled goat cheese
1 tablespoon minced fresh basil
1/4 teaspoon salt
1/4 teaspoon freshly ground black pepper

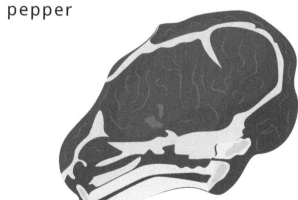

🌿 **DIRECTIONS**

1. In a large mixing bowl, combine the lamb, mushrooms, salt, and pepper, and mix well.
2. In a small bowl, mix the goat cheese and basil.
3. Form the lamb mixture into 4 patties, reserving about ½ cup of the mixture in the bowl. In each patty, make an indentation in the center and fill with 1 tablespoon of the goat cheese mixture. Use the reserved meat mixture to close the burgers. Press the meat firmly to hold together.
4. Heat the barbecue or a large skillet over medium-high heat. Add the burgers and cook for 5 to 7 minutes on each side, until cooked through. Serve.

Parmesan Golden Pork Chops

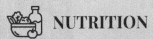

🕐 Preparation Time: 10 minutes
Cook Time: 25minutes

🍴 Servings: 4

🥗 **NUTRITION**

Calories -------------------- 333
Fat -------------------- 16.1g
Protein -------------------- 44.1g

 **INGREDIENTS**

4 bone-in, thin-cut pork chops
1/2 cup grated Parmesan cheese
3 garlic cloves, minced
1/4 teaspoon dried thyme
Nonstick cooking spray
2 tablespoons butter
1/4 teaspoon salt
Freshly ground black pepper, to taste

 DIRECTIONS

1. Preheat the oven to 400°F (205°C). Line a baking sheet with parchment paper and spray with nonstick cooking spray.
2. Arrange the pork chops on the prepared baking sheet so they do not overlap.
3. In a small bowl, combine the butter, Parmesan cheese, minced garlic, salt, dried thyme, and freshly ground black pepper. Mix well.
4. Press 2 tablespoons of the cheese mixture onto the top of each pork chop.
5. Bake in the preheated oven for 18 to 22 minutes, or until the pork is cooked through and its juices run clear.
6. Set the broiler to high, then broil the pork chops for 1 to 2 minutes to brown the tops.
7. Remove from the oven and let rest for a few minutes before serving.

Grilled Lemon Herbed Chicken

Preparation Time: 10 minutes
Cook Time: 15 minutes

Servings: 6

NUTRITION

Calories -------------------- 430
Fat ------------------- 19.2g
Sodium ------------------- 320mg
Carbs ------------------ 7.6g
Fiber ------------------ 1.3g
Sugar ------------------ 0.3g
Protein ------------------ 56.8g

INGREDIENTS

emon wedges (optional)
resh sprigs of thyme (optional)
/8 to 1/4 teaspoon ground black
epper
/4 teaspoon salt
/4 to 1/2 teaspoon crushed red
epper
teaspoon fresh rosemary
teaspoons snipped fresh thyme
tablespoon shredded lemon peel
cloves garlic, minced
/4 cup olive oil
skinless, boneless chicken breast
alves

DIRECTIONS

1. Place a chicken breast between 2 pieces of plastic wrap.
2. Pound lightly with a meat mallet until it is 1/8 inch thick.
3. Season the chicken with salt and pepper. Repeat the process for all chicken breasts. Set aside.
4. In a medium skillet, cook the garlic and shallots in 2 tablespoon hot oil until they are tender. Remove from the heat and add nuts, spinach and smoked mozzarella.
5. In another bowl, combine the parmesan cheese and bread crumbs. Add to the nut mixture.
6. Place 2 tablespoon of the filling on one side of the chicken breast. Fold the chicken breast then secure with wooden toothpicks.
7. Brush the chicken breasts with olive oil and coat with bread crumbs. Place the chicken seam side down and bake for 400 degrees Fahrenheit for 25 minutes.
8. Remove the toothpicks before serving.

Sesame Beef Kabobs

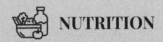
Preparation Time: 20 minutes
Cook Time: 18 minutes

Servings: 4

DIRECTIONS

1. Score the sides of the beef by making shallow diagonal cuts across the meat. Place it in a resealable plastic bag.

2. In a small bowl, mix together the sesame oil, soy sauce, coconut sugar, green onion, dry sherry (if using), minced garlic, sesame seeds, and crushed red pepper to create the marinade.

3. Pour the marinade over the beef in the plastic bag. Seal the bag and refrigerate for 4 to 24 hours.

4. Drain the beef and discard the marinade.

5. Preheat the grill to medium heat. Place the beef on the grill rack and cook directly over medium coals for about 14 minutes or until tender, turning occasionally.

6. Add the quartered sweet peppers and lime wedges to the grill during the last 4 minutes of cooking.

7. In a small saucepan, cook the pea pods in boiling water for 4 minutes. Drain and set aside.

8. Thread the beef pieces, sweet peppers, pea pods, and cherry tomatoes onto skewers.

9. Sprinkle the kabobs with sesame seeds and serve with lime wedges.

NUTRITION

Calories ------------------- 327
Fat ------------------ 24.3g
Sodium ------------------ 230mg
Carbs ------------------ 19.9g
Fiber ------------------ 4.4g
Sugar ------------------ 8.3g
Protein ------------------ 26.8g

INGREDIENTS

Sesame seeds
30 cherry tomatoes
3/4 cup fresh pea pods, trimmed
4 limes, cut into 8 wedges each
2 small orange or red sweet peppers, quartered
1/2 teaspoon crushed red pepper
1/2 teaspoon sesame seeds
2 cloves garlic, minced
1 1/2 teaspoons dry sherry (optional)
1 1/2 teaspoons coconut sugar
1 green onion, sliced
2 tablespoons sesame oil
2 tablespoons low-sodium soy sauce
12 ounces beef flank steak, fat trimmed

Spicy Citrus Sole

Preparation Time: 10 minutes
Cook Time: 10 minutes

Servings: 4

NUTRITION

Calories -------------------- 184
Total Fat ------------------ 5g
Cholesterol ------------------- 81mg
Sodium ------------------ 137mg
Total Carbohydrates -------- 0g
Sugars -------------------- 0g
Fiber -------------------- 0g
Protein ------------------ 32g

INGREDIENTS

1 teaspoon chili powder
1 teaspoon garlic powder
1/2 teaspoon lime zest
1/2 teaspoon lemon zest
1/4 teaspoon freshly ground black pepper
1/4 teaspoon smoked paprika
Pinch of sea salt
4 (6-ounce) sole fillets, patted dry
1 tablespoon extra-virgin olive oil
2 teaspoons freshly squeezed lime juice

DIRECTIONS

1. Preheat the oven to 450°F (230°C).
2. Line a baking sheet with aluminum foil and set it aside.
3. In a small bowl, stir together the chili powder, garlic powder, lime zest, lemon zest, black pepper, smoked paprika, and sea salt until well mixed.
4. Pat the fish fillets dry with paper towels, place them on the prepared baking sheet, and rub them lightly all over with the spice mixture.
5. Drizzle the olive oil and lime juice on top of the fish fillets.
6. Bake in the preheated oven for about 8 minutes, or until the fish flakes easily when pressed lightly with a fork. Serve immediately.

Simple Buttercup Squash Soup

Preparation Time: 15 minutes
Cook Time: 33 minutes

Servings: 6

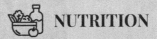 **NUTRITION**

Calories -------------------- 110
Total Fat ------------------- 5g
Protein -------------------- 1g

 INGREDIENTS

1 medium onion, chopped
11/2pounds (680 g) buttercup
squash, peeled, deseeded, and cut
into 1-inch chunks
4 cups vegetable broth
Ground nutmeg, to taste
2 tablespoons extra-virgin olive oil
1/2 teaspoon kosher salt
1/4 teaspoon ground white pepper

 DIRECTIONS

1. Heat the olive oil in a pot over medium-high heat until shimmering.
2. Add the chopped onion and saute for about 3 minutes or until translucent.
3. Add the buttercup squash, vegetable broth, salt, and white pepper. Stir to mix well and bring to a boil.
4. Reduce the heat to low and simmer for 30 minutes, or until the buttercup squash is soft.
5. Pour the soup into a food processor and pulse until pureed and creamy.
6. Pour the pureed soup into a large serving bowl, sprinkle with ground nutmeg, and serve immediately.

Chapter 3:

DINNER

Orange-Marinated Pork Tenderloin

 DIRECTIONS

1. In a bowl, blend together the orange juice, orange zest, minced garlic, soy sauce, grated ginger, and honey to make the marinade.
2. Pour the marinade into a resealable plastic bag and add the pork tenderloin. Remove as much air as possible and seal the bag. Marinate the pork in the refrigerator for 2 hours, turning the bag a few times to ensure even coating.
3. Preheat the oven to 400°F (200°C).
4. Remove the pork tenderloin from the marinade and discard the marinade.
5. Heat a large ovenproof skillet over medium-high heat and add the olive oil.
6. Sear the pork tenderloin on all sides until browned, about 5 minutes in total.
7. Transfer the skillet to the preheated oven and roast the pork for 25 minutes or until the internal temperature reaches 145°F (63°C).
8. Remove the skillet from the oven and let the pork rest for 10 minutes before slicing and serving.

Preparation Time: 2 minutes
Cook Time: 30 minutes

Servings: 4

NUTRITION

Calories -------------------- 228
Carbohydrates -------------------- 4g
Sugar -------------------- 3g

INGREDIENTS

1/4 cup freshly squeezed orange juice
2 teaspoons orange zest
2 teaspoons minced garlic
1 teaspoon low-sodium soy sauce
1 teaspoon grated fresh ginger
1 teaspoon honey
1 1/2pounds pork tenderloin roas
1 tablespoon extra-virgin olive oi

Strawberry-Arugula Salad

Preparation Time: 10 minutes
Cook Time: 10 minutes

Servings: 2

NUTRITION

Calories -------------------- 41
Protein -------------------- 0.2g
Fat -------------------- 0.4g
Carbohydrates ----------- 20g

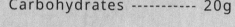 **INGREDIENTS**

1/4 cup fresh parsley leaves, chopped
2 cups arugula
1/2 cup strawberries, quartered
1/4 cup fresh basil leaves
3 tablespoons lemon vinaigrette
1/4 cup red onion, thinly sliced
Thinly sliced almonds (optional) for topping
Salt and pepper, to taste

 DIRECTIONS

1. In a salad bowl, toss together the parsley, arugula, and basil.
2. Add the lemon vinaigrette, strawberries, and red onion. Toss again to combine.
3. Season the salad with salt and pepper to taste.
4. Top with thinly sliced almonds, if desired.
5. Serve immediately and enjoy!

Roasted Mixed Vegetables

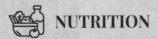

⏱ Preparation Time: 5 minutes
Cook Time:20 minutes

🍴 Servings: 4

🥗 **NUTRITION**

Calories ------------------- 70
Protein ------------------- 10g
Fat ------------------- 4g
Carbs ------------------- 1g

 INGREDIENTS

1/2 (8 ounces) package whole button mushrooms
1 (12 ounces) package cauliflower, carrot, and broccoli mix
1/4 teaspoon sea salt
Freshly ground black pepper, to taste
2 tablespoons extra virgin olive oil

 DIRECTIONS

1. Preheat your oven to 450°F (232°C).

2. In a mixing bowl, toss the vegetables with olive oil, sea salt, and pepper.

3. Spread the mixed veggies onto a baking sheet in a single layer.

4. Bake for 20 minutes, or until the vegetables are tender and slightly browned.

5. Serve and enjoy!

Spaghetti Puttanesca

Preparation Time: 20 minutes
Cook Time: 35 minutes

Servings: 6

NUTRITION

Calories -------------------- 200
Total Fat -------------------- 5g
Cholesterol -------------------- 28mg
Sodium -------------------- 88mg
Total Carbohydrates ----------------
--- 35g
Sugar -------------------- 8g
Fiber -------------------- 4g
Protein -------------------- 7g

INGREDIENTS

tablespoon extra-virgin olive oil
sweet onion, chopped
celery stalks, chopped
teaspoons minced garlic
(28-ounce) cans sodium-free
diced tomatoes
tablespoons chopped fresh basil
tablespoon chopped fresh
oregano
1/2 teaspoon red pepper flakes
1/2 cup quartered, pitted Kalamata
olives
1/4 cup freshly squeezed lemon
juice
ounces whole-wheat spaghetti

DIRECTIONS

1. Place a large saucepan over medium-high heat and add the olive oil.
2. Saute the onion, celery, and garlic until they are translucent, about 3 minutes.
3. Add the tomatoes, basil, oregano, and red pepper flakes, and bring the sauce to a boil, stirring occasionally.
4. Reduce the heat to low and simmer for 20 minutes, stirring occasionally.
5. Stir in the olives and lemon juice, and remove the saucepan from the heat.
6. Cook the pasta according to the package instructions.
7. Spoon the sauce over the pasta and serve.

Lemon Cauliflower and Pine Nuts

Preparation Time: 5 minutes
Cook Time: 20 minutes

Servings: 4

NUTRITION

Calories -------------------- 60
Protein -------------------- 4g
Fat -------------------- 0g
Carbs ------------------- 8g

 ## DIRECTIONS

1. Preheat your oven to 400°F (205°C).
2. In a large bowl, combine all the ingredients, ensuring the cauliflower florets are evenly coated with the olive oil, lemon zest, lemon juice, salt, pepper, parsley, and pine nuts.
3. Spread the mixture onto a baking sheet in a single layer.
4. Bake for 20 minutes or until the cauliflower is tender and lightly browned.
5. Serve and enjoy!

INGREDIENTS

1 teaspoon lemon zest
1/4 teaspoon sea salt
1 (10 ounces) package cauliflower florets
2 tablespoons extra virgin olive oil
2 tablespoons pine nuts
1 tablespoon fresh flat-leaf parsley, chopped
1 1/2 teaspoons lemon juice
1/4 teaspoon freshly ground black pepper

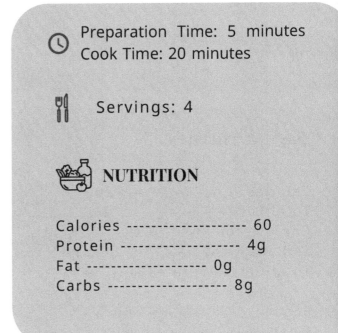

Beef Tenderloin and Avocado Cream

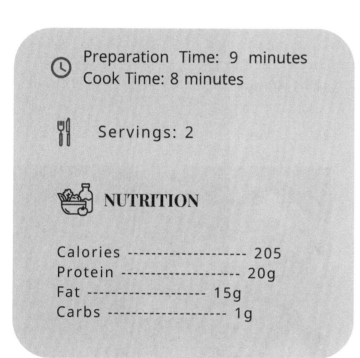

Preparation Time: 9 minutes
Cook Time: 8 minutes

Servings: 2

NUTRITION

Calories -------------------- 205
Protein -------------------- 20g
Fat -------------------- 15g
Carbs -------------------- 1g

INGREDIENTS

1 teaspoon mustard
2 (6 ounces) beef steaks
1/4 cup sour cream
2 teaspoons fresh lemon juice
1/3 avocado
1 tablespoon olive oil
Sea salt and freshly ground black pepper, to taste

 **DIRECTIONS**

1. Preheat your oven to 450°F (232°C).
2. Sprinkle the beef steaks with salt and pepper.
3. In a small bowl, mix the mustard and olive oil. Spread this mixture over the steaks.
4. Heat a skillet over medium-high heat. Place the steaks in the skillet and sear for 3 minutes on each side.
5. Transfer the steaks to a baking sheet and bake in the preheated oven for 6 minutes, or until desired doneness.
6. While the steaks are baking, blend the avocado, lemon juice, and sour cream until smooth to create the avocado cream.
7. Serve the steaks topped with the avocado cream and enjoy!

Lime-Parsley Lamb Cutlets

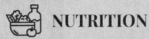

🕐 Preparation Time: 4 minutes
Cook Time:10 minutes

🍴 Servings: 4

🥗 **NUTRITION**

Calories -------------------- 413
Carbohydrates -------------------- 1g
Protein ------------------- 31g

 **INGREDIENTS**

1/4 cup extra-virgin olive oil
1/4 cup freshly squeezed lime juice
2 tablespoons lime zest
2 tablespoons chopped fresh parsley
12 lamb cutlets (about 1½ pounds total)
Salt and freshly ground black pepper, to taste

 DIRECTIONS

1. In a bowl, mix together the olive oil, lime juice, lime zest, parsley, salt, and pepper.
2. Pour the marinade into a resealable plastic bag.
3. Add the lamb cutlets to the bag, remove as much air as possible, and seal the bag.
4. Marinate the lamb in the refrigerator for about 4 hours, turning the bag several times to ensure even marination.
5. Preheat the oven to broil.
6. Remove the cutlets from the bag and arrange them on an aluminum foil-lined baking sheet. Discard the marinade.
7. Broil the cutlets for 4 minutes per side for medium doneness.
8. Let the cutlets rest for 5 minutes before serving.

Spiced Lamb Stew

 Preparation Time: 20 minutes
Cook Time: 2 hours, 15inutes

 Servings: 6

NUTRITION

Calories -------------------- 200
Total Fat ------------------ 5g
Cholesterol -------------------- 28mg
Sodium ------------------ 88mg
Total Carbohydrates ----------------
--- 35g
Sugar -------------------- 8g
Fiber ------------------ 4g
Protein -------------------- 7g

INGREDIENTS

 tablespoons extra-virgin olive oil
 1/2pounds lamb shoulder, cut
nto 1-inch chunks
/2sweet onion, chopped
 tablespoon grated fresh ginger
 teaspoons minced garlic
 teaspoon ground cinnamon
 teaspoon ground cumin
/4 teaspoon ground cloves
 sweet potatoes, peeled and diced
 cups low-sodium beef broth
ea salt, to taste
reshly ground black pepper, to
aste
 teaspoons chopped fresh parsley,
or garnish

DIRECTIONS

1. Preheat the oven to 300°F.
2. Place a large ovenproof skillet over medium-high heat and add the olive oil.
3. Brown the lamb, stirring occasionally, for about 6 minutes.
4. Add the onion, ginger, garlic, cinnamon, cumin, and cloves, and sauté for 5 minutes until fragrant.
5. Add the sweet potatoes and beef broth and bring the stew to a boil.
6. Cover the skillet and transfer to the oven. Braise, stirring occasionally, until the lamb is very tender, about 2 hours.
7. Remove the stew from the oven and season with salt and pepper to taste.
8. Serve garnished with chopped fresh parsley.

Mediterranean Steak Sandwiches

Preparation Time: 1 hour
Cook Time: 10 minutes

Servings: 4

NUTRITION

Calories -------------------- 60
Protein ------------------- 4g
Fat ------------------- 0g
Carbs ------------------- 8g

 **DIRECTIONS**

1. Scourge olive oil, balsamic vinegar, garlic, lemon juice, oregano, and parsley
2. Add the steak to the bowl, turning to coat it completely.
3. Marinate the steak for 1 hour in the refrigerator, turning it over several times.
4. Preheat the broiler. Line a baking sheet with aluminum foil.
5. Put steak out of the bowl and discard the marinade.
6. Situate steak on the baking sheet and broil for 5 minutes per side for medium.
7. Set aside for 10 minutes before slicing.
8. Stuff the pitas with the sliced steak, lettuce, onion, tomato, and feta.

 INGREDIENTS

2 tablespoons extra-virgin olive oil
2 tablespoons balsamic vinegar
2 teaspoons garlic
2 teaspoons lemon juice
2 teaspoons fresh oregano
1 teaspoon fresh parsley
1-pound flank steak
4 whole-wheat pitas
2 cups shredded lettuce
1 red onion, thinly sliced
1 tomato, chopped
1 ounce low-sodium feta cheese

Roasted Beef with Peppercorn Sauce

Preparation Time: 10 minutes
Cook Time: 90 minutes

Servings: 4

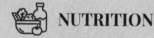

NUTRITION

Calories -------------------- 330
Carbohydrates -------------------- 4g
Protein -------------------- 36g

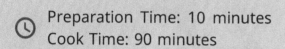

INGREDIENTS

1 1/2 pounds top rump beef roast
3 teaspoons extra-virgin olive oil
3 shallots, minced
2 teaspoons minced garlic
1 tablespoon green peppercorns
2 tablespoons dry sherry
2 tablespoons all-purpose flour
1 cup sodium-free beef broth

DIRECTIONS

1. Heat the oven to 300°F.
2. Season the roast with salt and pepper.
3. Position huge skillet over medium-high heat and add 2 teaspoons of olive oil.
4. Brown the beef on all sides, about 10 minutes in total, and transfer the roast to a baking dish.
5. Roast until desired doneness, about 1½ hours for medium. When the roast has been in the oven for 1 hour, start the sauce.
6. In a medium saucepan over medium-high heat, saute the shallots in the remaining 1 teaspoon of olive oil until translucent, about 4 minutes.
7. Stir in the garlic and peppercorns, and cook for another minute. Whisk in the sherry to deglaze the pan.
8. Whisk in the flour to form a thick paste, cooking for 1 minute and stirring constantly.
9. Fill in the beef broth and whisk for 4 minutes. Season the sauce.
Serve the beef with a generous spoonful of sauce.

Chapter 4:
SEAFOOD

Orange-Infused Scallops

Preparation Time: 10 minutes
Cook Time:10 minutes

Servings: 4

 NUTRITION

Calories -------------------- 267	Total Carbohydrates ------------ 8g
Total Fat ------------------- 8g	Sugar ------------------- 1g
Cholesterol ------------------- 74mg	Fiber ------------------- 0g
Sodium ------------------ 361mg	Protein ------------------- 38g

INGREDIENTS

2 pounds sea scallops
Sea salt
Freshly ground black pepper
2 tablespoons extra-virgin olive oil
1 tablespoon minced garlic
1/4cup freshly squeezed orange juice
1 teaspoon orange zest
2 teaspoons chopped fresh thyme, for garnish

 DIRECTIONS

1. Clean the scallops and pat them dry with paper towels. Season them lightly with sea salt and freshly ground black pepper.
2. Place a large skillet over medium-high heat and add the extra-virgin olive oil.
3. Saute the minced garlic until it is softened and translucent, about 3 minutes.
4. Add the scallops to the skillet and cook until they are lightly seared and just cooked through, turning once, about 4 minutes per side.
5. Transfer the scallops to a plate, cover to keep warm, and set them aside.
6. Add the freshly squeezed orange juice and orange zest to the skillet, stirring to scrape up any cooked bits.
7. Spoon the orange sauce over the scallops and serve, garnished with chopped fresh thyme.

Shrimp with Tomatoes and Feta

 Preparation Time: 10 minutes
Cook Time: 30 minutes

 Servings:4

NUTRITION

Calories -------------------- 306
Total Fat -------------------- 11g
Cholesterol --------------------
272mg
Sodium -------------------- 502mg
Total Carbohydrates ----------------
--- 12g
Sugar -------------------- 5g
Fiber -------------------- 3g
Protein -------------------- 39g

INGREDIENTS

3 tomatoes, coarsely chopped
1/2cup chopped sun-dried tomatoes
2 teaspoons minced garlic
2 teaspoons extra-virgin olive oil
1 teaspoon chopped fresh oregano
Freshly ground black pepper, to
taste
1 1/2 pounds (16–20 count) shrimp,
peeled, deveined, tails removed
4 teaspoons freshly squeezed
lemon juice
1/2cup low-sodium feta cheese,
crumbled

DIRECTIONS

1. Preheat the oven to 450°F.
2. In a medium bowl, toss the tomatoes, sun-dried tomatoes, garlic olive oil, and oregano until well combined. Season lightly with freshly ground black pepper.
3. Transfer the tomato mixture to a 9-by-13-inch glass baking dish.
4. Bake until the tomatoes are softened, about 15 minutes.
5. Stir the shrimp and lemon juice into the hot tomato mixture and top evenly with the crumbled feta.
6. Bake until the shrimp are cooked through, about 15 minutes more.

Crab Cakes with Honeydew Melon Salsa

DIRECTIONS

1. In a small bowl, stir together the honeydew melon, scallion, bell pepper, and thyme.

2. Season the salsa with sea salt and freshly ground black pepper and set aside.

1. In a medium bowl, mix together the crabmeat, red onion, panko bread crumbs, parsley, lemon zest, and egg until very well combined.

2. Divide the crab mixture into 8 equal portions and form them into patties about ¾-inch thick.

3. Chill the crab cakes in the refrigerator for at least 1 hour to firm them up.

4. Dredge the chilled crab cakes in whole-wheat flour until lightly coated, shaking off any excess flour.

5. Place a large skillet over medium heat and lightly coat it with nonstick cooking spray.

6. Cook the crab cakes until they are golden brown, turning once, about 5 minutes per side.

7. Serve the crab cakes warm with the honeydew melon salsa.

Preparation Time: 30 minutes
Cook Time: 10 minutes

Servings: 4

NUTRITION

Calories -------------------- 232
Total Fat ------------------- 3g
Cholesterol -------------------- 137mg
Sodium ------------------- 767mg
Total Carbohydrates ------------------- 18g
Sugar ------------------- 6g
Fiber ------------------- 2g
Protein ------------------- 32g

INGREDIENTS

1 cup finely chopped honeydew melon
1 scallion, white and green parts, finely chopped
1 red bell pepper, seeded, finely chopped
1 teaspoon chopped fresh thyme
Pinch sea salt
Pinch freshly ground black pepper
1 pound lump crabmeat, drained and picked over
1/4 cup finely chopped red onion
1/4cup panko bread crumbs
1 tablespoon chopped fresh parsley
1 teaspoon lemon zest
1 egg
1/4cup whole-wheat flour
Nonstick cooking spray

Seafood Stew

Preparation Time: 20 minutes
Cook Time: 30 minutes

 Servings: 6

 NUTRITION

Calories -------------------- 248
Total Fat -------------------- 7g
Cholesterol --------------------
103mg
Sodium ------------------ 577mg
Total Carbohydrates ----------------
--- 19g
Sugar -------------------- 7g
Fiber -------------------- 2g
Protein ------------------- 28g

INGREDIENTS

1 tablespoon extra-virgin olive oil
1 sweet onion, chopped
2 teaspoons minced garlic
3 celery stalks, chopped
2 carrots, peeled and chopped
1 (28-ounce) can sodium-free diced
tomatoes, undrained
3 cups low-sodium chicken broth
1/2 cup clam juice
1/4 cup dry white wine
2 teaspoons chopped fresh basil
2 teaspoons chopped fresh oregano
2 (4-ounce) haddock fillets, cut into
1-inch chunks
1 pound mussels, scrubbed,
debearded
8 ounces (16–20 count) shrimp,
peeled, deveined, quartered
Sea salt
Freshly ground black pepper
2 tablespoons chopped fresh
parsley

DIRECTIONS

1. Place a large saucepan over medium-high heat and add the olive oil.
2. Saute the onion and garlic until softened and translucent, about 3 minutes.
3. Stir in the celery and carrots and sauté for 4 minutes.
4. Stir in the tomatoes, chicken broth, clam juice, white wine, basil, and oregano.
5. Bring the sauce to a boil, then reduce the heat to low. Simmer for 15 minutes.
6. Add the fish and mussels, cover, and cook until the mussels open, about 5 minutes.
7. Discard any unopened mussels. Add the shrimp to the pan and cook until the shrimp are opaque, about 2 minutes.

Basil-Parmesan Crusted Salmon

Preparation Time: 5 minutes
Cook Time:15 minutes

Servings: 4

NUTRITION

Calories	267	Total Carbohydrates	8g
Total Fat	8g	Sugar	1g
Cholesterol	74mg	Fiber	0g
Sodium	361mg	Protein	38g

INGREDIENTS

Grated Parmesan: 3 tablespoons
Skinless four salmon fillets
Salt: 1/4 teaspoon
Freshly ground black pepper
Low-fat mayonnaise: 3 tablespoons
Basil leaves, chopped
Half lemon

DIRECTIONS

1. Let the air fryer preheat to 400F. Spray the basket with olive oil.
2. With salt, pepper, and lemon juice, season the salmon.
3. In a bowl, mix two tablespoons of Parmesan cheese with mayonnaise and basil leaves.
4. Add this mix and more parmesan on top of salmon and cook for seven minutes or until fully cooked. Serve hot.

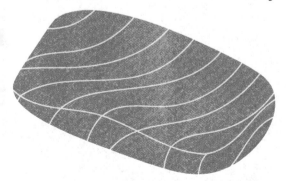

Coconut Shrimp

Preparation Time: 10 minutes
Cook Time: 30 minutes

Servings:4

NUTRITION

Calories -------------------- 340
Protein -------------------- 25g
Fat ------------------- 16g

INGREDIENTS

1/2 cup crushed pork rinds
4 cups jumbo shrimp, deveined
1/2cup coconut flakes (preferably unsweetened)
2 eggs
1/2 cup coconut flour
Oil of your choice for frying (at least half-inch in the pan)
Freshly ground black pepper and kosher salt to taste
2-3 tablespoons powdered sugar substitute
3 tablespoons mayonnaise
1/2 cup sour cream
1/4teaspoon coconut extract (or to taste)
3 tablespoons coconut cream
1/4 teaspoon pineapple flavoring (or to taste)
3 tablespoons coconut flakes (preferably unsweetened, optional)

DIRECTIONS

1.   Mix all the sauce ingredients in a small bowl.
2.   Combine well and refrigerate until ready to serve.
Shrimp:
1. Whip the eggs in a deep bowl.
2. In a small, shallow bowl, combine the crushed pork rinds, coconut flou sea salt, coconut flakes, and freshly ground black pepper.
3. Dip each shrimp into the egg mixture, then coat with the coconut flour blend.
4. Place the coated shrimp on a clea plate or directly in the air fryer basket.
5. Arrange the battered shrimp in a single layer in your air fryer basket.
6. Spritz the shrimp with oil and coc for 8-10 minutes at 360°F, flipping them halfway through.

Tomato and Roasted Cod

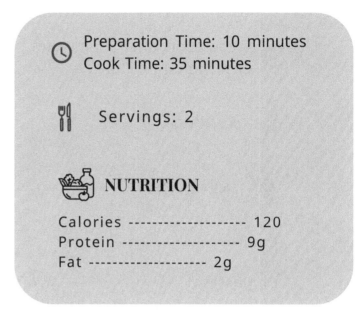

Preparation Time: 10 minutes
Cook Time: 35 minutes

Servings: 2

NUTRITION

Calories -------------------- 120
Protein ------------------- 9g
Fat -------------------- 2g

 DIRECTIONS

1. Preheat your oven to 400°F.
2. In a mixing bowl, combine half of the cherry tomatoes, sliced onion, grated orange rind, extra virgin olive oil, dried thyme, and 1/8 teaspoon each of salt and pepper.
3. Spread the mixture on a baking pan and roast in the oven for 25 minutes.
4. Remove the pan from the oven.
5. Arrange the cod fillets on the pan.
6. Season the cod fillets with the remaining 1/8 teaspoon each of salt and pepper.
7. Top the cod fillets with the reserved tomato mixture.
8. Return the pan to the oven and bake for an additional 10 minutes, or until the fish is cooked through and flakes easily with a fork.

 INGREDIENTS

2 (4-ounce) cod fillets
1 cup cherry tomatoes, halved
2/3 cup onion, sliced
2 teaspoons orange rind, grated
1 tablespoon extra virgin olive oil
1 teaspoon dried thyme
1/4 teaspoon salt, divided
1/4 teaspoon freshly ground black pepper, divided

Spicy Citrus Sole

 Preparation Time: 10 minutes
Cook Time:10 minutes

Servings: 4

NUTRITION

Calories -------------------- 184
Total Fat -------------------- 5g
Cholesterol -------------------- 81mg
Sodium -------------------- 137mg
Total Carbohydrates ------------ 0g
Sugar -------------------- 0g
Fiber -------------------- 0g
Protein -------------------- 32g

 INGREDIENTS

1 teaspoon chili powder

1 teaspoon garlic powder

1/2 teaspoon lime zest

1/2 teaspoon lemon zest

1/4 teaspoon freshly ground black
pepper

1/4 teaspoon smoked paprika

Pinch sea salt

4 (6-ounce) sole fillets, patted dry

1 tablespoon extra-virgin olive oil

2 teaspoons freshly squeezed lime
juice

 DIRECTIONS

1. Preheat the oven to 450°F.
2. Line a baking sheet with
aluminum foil and set it aside.
3. In a small bowl, stir together
the chili powder, garlic powder,
lime zest, lemon zest, pepper,
paprika, and salt until well mixed.
4. Pat the fish fillets dry with
paper towels, place them on the
baking sheet, and rub them lightly
all over with the spice mixture.
5. Drizzle the olive oil and lime
juice on the top of the fish.
6. Bake until the fish flakes when
pressed lightly with a fork, about
8 minutes. Serve immediately.

Haddock with Creamy Cucumber Sauce

🕐	Preparation Time: 10 minutes Cook Time:10 minutes	
🍴	Servings: 4	

 NUTRITION

Calories ------------------ 164	Total Carbohydrates ------------ 4g
Total Fat ------------------ 2g	Sugar ------------------ 3g
Cholesterol ------------------ 82mg	Fiber ------------------ 0g
Sodium ------------------ 104mg	Protein ------------------ 27g

INGREDIENTS

1/4 cup 2 percent plain Greek yogurt
1/2 English cucumber, grated, liquid squeezed out
1/2 scallion, white and green parts, finely chopped
2 teaspoons chopped fresh mint
1 teaspoon honey
Sea salt
4 (5-ounce) haddock fillets
Freshly ground black pepper
Nonstick cooking spray

 DIRECTIONS

1. In a small bowl, stir together the yogurt, cucumber, scallion, mint, honey, and a pinch of salt. Set it aside.
2. Pat the fish fillets dry with paper towels and season them lightly with salt and pepper.
3. Place a large skillet over medium-high heat and spray lightly with cooking spray.
4. Cook the haddock, turning once, until it is just cooked through, about 5 minutes per side.
5. Remove the fish from the heat and transfer to plates.
6. Serve topped with the cucumber sauce.

Herb-Crusted Halibut

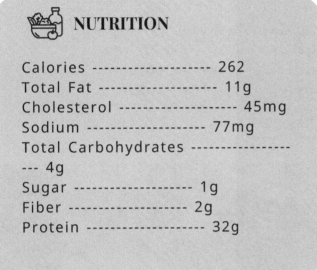

Preparation Time: 10 minutes
Cook Time: 20 minutes

Servings:4

NUTRITION

Calories -------------------- 262
Total Fat ------------------- 11g
Cholesterol ------------------ 45mg
Sodium ------------------- 77mg
Total Carbohydrates ----------------
--- 4g
Sugar ------------------- 1g
Fiber ------------------- 2g
Protein ------------------- 32g

INGREDIENTS

4 (5-ounce) halibut fillets
Extra-virgin olive oil, for brushing
1/2 cup coarsely ground unsalted
pistachios
1 tablespoon chopped fresh parsley
1 teaspoon chopped fresh thyme
1 teaspoon chopped fresh basil
Pinch sea salt
Pinch freshly ground black pepper

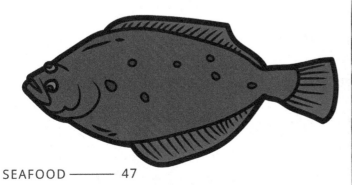

DIRECTIONS

1. Preheat the oven to 350°F.
2. Line a baking sheet with parchment paper.
3. Pat the halibut fillets dry with a paper towel and place them on the baking sheet.
4. Brush the halibut generously with olive oil.
5. In a small bowl, stir together the pistachios, parsley, thyme, basil, salt and pepper.
6. Spoon the nut and herb mixture evenly on the fish, spreading it out s the tops of the fillets are covered.
7. Bake the halibut until it flakes when pressed with a fork, about 20 minutes.
8. Serve immediately.

Chapter 5:

APPETIZERS

Chicken Tikka Masala

Preparation Time: 5 minutes
Cook Time: 15 minutes

Servings: 2

 NUTRITION

Calories -------------------- 200
Fat -------------------- 10g
Protein -------------------- 26g

 INGREDIENTS

1/2 lb. chicken breasts
1/4 cup onion
1.5 tsp extra virgin olive oil
1 (14.5-oz) can tomatoes
1 tsp ginger
1 tsp fresh lemon juice
1/3 cup plain Greek yogurt (fat-free)
1 tbsp garam masala
1/4 tsp salt
1/4 tsp pepper

DIRECTIONS

1. Flavor chicken cut into 1-inch cubes with 1.5 tsp garam masala, 1/8 tsp salt, and pepper.
2. Cook chicken and diced onion for 4 to 5 minutes.
3. Add diced tomatoes, grated ginger, 1.5 tsp garam masala, and 1/8 tsp salt. Cook for 8 to 10 minutes.
4. Add lemon juice and yogurt until blended.

Turkey Loaf

⏰ Preparation Time: 10 minutes
Cook Time:50 minutes

🍴 Servings: 4

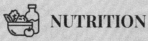 **NUTRITION**

Calories ------------------- 161
Protein ------------------ 20g
Fat ------------------- 8g

 INGREDIENTS

1/2 lb. 93% lean ground turkey
1/3 cup panko breadcrumbs
1/2 cup green onion
1 egg
1/2 cup green bell pepper
1 tbsp ketchup
1/4 cup sauce (Picante)
1/2 tsp cumin (ground

 DIRECTIONS

1. Preheat oven to 350°F.
2. In a bowl, mix lean ground turkey, 3 tbsp Picante sauce, panko breadcrumbs, egg, chopped green onion, chopped green bell pepper, and ground cumin. Mix well.
3. Put the mixture into a baking sheet and shape it into an oval about 1.5 inches thick.Bake for 45 minutes.
4. Mix the remaining Picante sauce and ketchup. Apply the mixture over the loaf.
5. Bake for an additional 5 minutes.
6. Let it stand for 5 minutes before serving.

Aromatic Toasted Pumpkin Seeds

 Preparation Time: 5 minutes
Cook Time: 45 minutes

 Servings:4

 NUTRITION

Calories -------------------- 202
Carbohydrates --------------------
5.1g
Fiber -------------------- 2.3g

 DIRECTIONS

1. Preheat the oven to 300°F (150°C).
2. In a bowl, combine the pumpkin seeds with cinnamon, stevia, canola oil, and salt. Stir well to mix.
3. Spread the seeds in a single layer on a baking sheet.
4. Place the baking sheet in the preheated oven and bake for 45 minutes or until the seeds are well toasted and fragrant. Shake the sheet twice during baking to ensure even toasting.
5. Once toasted, remove from the oven and let cool slightly.
6. Serve immediately.

INGREDIENTS

1 cup pumpkin seeds
1 teaspoon cinnamon
2 packets stevia
1 tablespoon canola oil
1/4 teaspoon sea salt

Bacon-Wrapped Shrimps

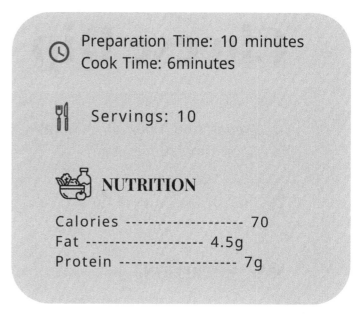

Preparation Time: 10 minutes
Cook Time: 6minutes

Servings: 10

NUTRITION

Calories -------------------- 70
Fat ------------------- 4.5g
Protein -------------------- 7g

INGREDIENTS

20 shrimps, peeled and deveined

7 slices bacon

4 leaves romaine lettuce

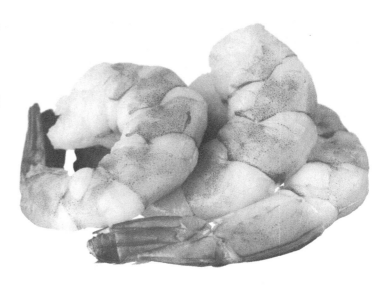

DIRECTIONS

1. Preheat the oven to 205°C (400°F).
2. Wrap each shrimp with a strip of bacon.
3. Arrange the bacon-wrapped shrimps seam side down on a baking sheet, ensuring they are in a single layer.
4. Broil the shrimps in the preheated oven for 6 minutes, flipping them halfway through the cooking time.
5. Once cooked, remove from the oven.
Serve the bacon-wrapped shrimps on romaine lettuce leaves

Mexican Black Bean and Cheese Dip

(L) Preparation Time: 45 minutes
Cook Time:20 minutes

(fork icon) Servings: 14

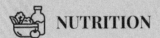 NUTRITION

Calories -------------------- 138
Total Fat -------------------- 1.7g
- Saturated Fat --------------------
0.2g
- Monounsaturated Fat -------------
------- 0.5g
- Polyunsaturated Fat ---------------
----- 0.7g
Cholesterol -------------------- 2mg
Sodium -------------------- 153mg
Carbohydrate --------------------
21.8g
- Dietary Fiber --------------------
7.7g
- Sugars ------------------- 2.2g
- Starches -------------------- 11.1g
Protein -------------------- 9.5g

INGREDIENTS

1 cup chopped yellow onion
1 tablespoon canola oil
1 large clove garlic, minced
4 (15.5-ounce) cans low-sodium
black beans, rinsed and drained
1 cup water
3 ounces fat-free cream cheese
(about 1/3 of an 8-ounce package)
1/3 cup shredded mild or sharp
reduced-fat, reduced-sodium
Cheddar cheese
2 tablespoons sliced scallions,
green part only
2 tablespoons pickled jalapeno
pepper slices, optional

DIRECTIONS

1. In a medium saucepan, saute
the onion in the canola oil over
medium heat until soft. Add the
garlic and saute for another
minute, stirring often.
2. Add the beans and water; stir
until well mixed. Reduce heat to
low, cover, and simmer for 30
minutes, stirring occasionally. If
the water cooks off, add more, 2
tablespoons at a time, to prevent
the beans from burning.
3. Stir in 1/3 cup water, and mix
with a wooden spoon so the beans
break apart and the mixture
becomes creamy.
4. Preheat oven to 375 degrees F
(190 degrees C).
5. Spoon the bean mixture into a
food processor and process for 30
seconds, or until smooth.
6. Spoon 1/3 of the bean mixture
into an 8-inch round casserole
that is at least 3 inches high and
spread evenly.
7. Scatter bits of the cream
cheese on top of the bean layer.
Spoon the remaining bean mixture
over the cream cheese layer and
spread evenly so that all of the
cream cheese is covered.
8. Sprinkle with the Cheddar
cheese and bake for 20 minutes.

Mango and Jicama Salad

Preparation Time: 15 minutes
Cook Time:0 minutes

Servings: 4

NUTRITION

Calories ------------------- 143
Carbohydrates ------------------- 20g
Cholesterol ------------------- 0mg

Fiber ------------------- 3g
Sugar ------------------- 1.6g
Fat ------------------- 7g
Protein ------------------- 1g
Sodium ------------------- 78mg

INGREDIENTS

1 jicama, peeled
1 mango, peeled
1 teaspoon ginger root, minced
1/3 cup chives, minced
1/2 cup cilantro, chopped
1/4 cup canola oil
1/2 cup white wine vinegar
2 tablespoons lime juice
1/4 cup honey
1/8 teaspoon pepper
1/4 teaspoon salt

 ## DIRECTIONS

1. Whisk together the vinegar, honey, canola oil, minced ginger root, pepper, and salt in a bowl to make the dressing.
2. Cut the mango and jicama into matchstick-sized pieces and place them in a large bowl.
3. Toss the mango and jicama with the lime juice to coat.
4. Add the dressing, minced chives, and chopped cilantro to the bowl. Toss well to combine.
5. Serve immediately or refrigerate until ready to serve.

Shrimp Diane

 Servings:4

NUTRITION

Calories -------------------- 167
Total Fat -------------------- 3.9g
Saturated Fat ---------- 0.3g
Monounsaturated Fat ----- 1.2g
Polyunsaturated Fat ------ 1.5g
Cholesterol -------- 134mg
Sodium -------------------- 206mg
Carbohydrate --------
Dietary Fiber -------- 0.7g
Sugars -------------------- 0.6g
Starches -------------------- 4.8g
Protein -------------------- 19.5g

INGREDIENTS

1 teaspoon canola oil
1 teaspoon margarine
2 tablespoons minced shallots
1 cup thinly sliced white
mushrooms
16 jumbo shrimp, peeled and
deveined (about 1 pound)
1/4 cup dry white wine
1/2 teaspoon ground cayenne
pepper
1/8 teaspoon freshly ground black
pepper
Pinch salt substitute
2 tablespoons sliced scallions
1 tablespoon cream sherry
4 1/2-inch-thick slices Italian bread
Canola or olive oil cooking spray
2 tablespoons chopped fresh
parsley

 DIRECTIONS

1. Preheat the oven to 400 degrees (200 degrees C).
2. In a large nonstick skillet, heat the oil and margarine over medium heat until the margarine melts. Add the shallots and saute for 1 minute.
3. Add the mushrooms and saute until they become tender. Add the shrimp, wine, cayenne pepper, black pepper, salt substitute, scallions, and sherry. Cover and cook, stirring occasionally, until the shrimp become pink and firm to touch, about 5 minutes.
4. Meanwhile, arrange the bread slices on a baking sheet and spray lightly with cooking spray; bake until just crisp.
5. Stir half the parsley into the shrimp, then divide equally among 4 dinner plates. Sprinkle with the remaining parsley and serve with a slice of warm bread on the side of th plate.

Easy Caprese Skewers

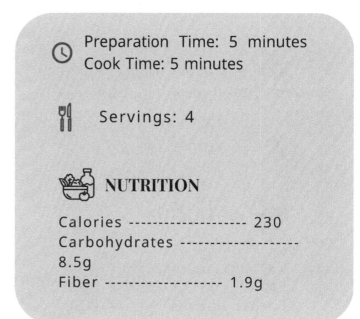

Preparation Time: 5 minutes
Cook Time: 5 minutes

Servings: 4

NUTRITION

Calories -------------------- 230
Carbohydrates -------------------- 8.5g
Fiber -------------------- 1.9g

DIRECTIONS

1. Thread the tomatoes, cheese, and basil leaves alternately through the skewers.
2. Place the skewers on a large plate.
3. Drizzle the Italian Vinaigrette over the skewers.
4. Serve immediately.

INGREDIENTS

12 cherry tomatoes
8 (1-inch) pieces Mozzarella cheese
12 basil leaves
1/4 cup Italian Vinaigrette, for serving

Mushroom Pasta

 Preparation Time: 5minutes
Cook Time:4 minutes

 Servings: 14

NUTRITION

Calories -------------------- 300
Fat ------------------- 1g
Carbohydrates -----------15g

INGREDIENTS

4 oz whole-grain linguine
1 tsp extra virgin olive oil
1/2 cup light sauce
2 tbsp green onion, finely chopped
1 (8-oz) package mushrooms, sliced
1 clove garlic, minced
1/8 tsp salt
1/8 tsp pepper

DIRECTIONS

1. Cook the linguine according to package directions. Drain and set aside.
2. In a skillet, heat the olive oil over medium heat. Add the sliced mushrooms and cook for about 4 minutes until they are tender.
3. Stir in the minced garlic, salt, and pepper. Cook for an additional 2 minutes.
4. Meanwhile, heat the light sauce until warmed through.
5. To serve, top the cooked pasta with the mushroom mixture, then pour the heated sauce over it.
6. Garnish with finely chopped green onion.

Kale Chips

Preparation Time: 10 minutes
Cook Time:14 minutes

Servings: 4

 NUTRITION

Calories -------------------- 136
Carbohydrates -------------------- 3g
Fiber -------------------- 1.1g

INGREDIENTS

1 (8-ounce) bunch kale
1 tablespoon extra-virgin olive oil
1/4 teaspoon garlic powder
Pinch of cayenne pepper, to taste
1/2 teaspoon sea salt, or to taste

 DIRECTIONS

1. Preheat the oven to 180°C (350°F). Line two baking sheets with parchment paper.
2. Wash the kale and remove the tough stems. Tear the leaves into bite-sized pieces.
3. In a large bowl, toss the kale with olive oil, garlic powder, cayenne pepper, and sea salt until well coated.
4. Spread the kale in a single layer on one of the prepared baking sheets.
5. Bake for 7 minutes, then remove the baking sheet from the oven and carefully transfer the kale to the second baking sheet, spreading it into a single layer.
6. Return the baking sheet to the oven and bake for an additional 7 minutes, or until the kale is crispy and lightly browned.
7. Remove from the oven and let cool slightly before serving.

Chapter 6:

SOUP

Italian Veggie Soup

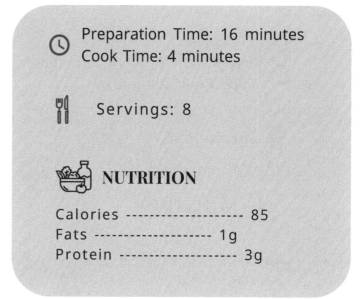

Preparation Time: 16 minutes
Cook Time: 4 minutes

Servings: 8

NUTRITION

Calories -------------------- 85
Fats ------------------- 1g
Protein -------------------- 3g

INGREDIENTS

4 cups cabbage, chopped
1 cup green beans, sliced into 1-inch pieces
2 cups fresh spinach, chopped
1 small onion, diced
2 green bell peppers, diced
2 celery stalks, diced
1 (28-ounce) can low-sodium diced tomatoes
6 cups low-sodium vegetable broth
1 tablespoon parsley
2 tablespoons tomato paste
1 1/2 teaspoons Italian seasoning
2 bay leaves
2 cloves garlic, finely diced
1 tablespoon basil
Pepper to taste

DIRECTIONS

1. Add the cabbage, green beans, onion, green bell peppers, celery, and garlic to a crockpot.
2. Pour in the diced tomatoes, tomato paste, and vegetable broth.
3. Add the bay leaves, Italian seasoning, and pepper. Stir to combine.
4. Cover with the pot lid and cook on high for 4 hours.
5. After 4 hours, add the spinach, parsley, and basil. Stir and cook for an additional 5 minutes.
6. Remove the bay leaves before serving.

Pea and Potato Soup

 Preparation Time: 10 minutes
Cook Time: 30 minutes

Servings: 2

NUTRITION

Calories -------------------- 259
Saturated Fat ----------- 2.8g
Net Carbs ------------------- 15g
Protein ------------------- 32g
Sugar ------------------- 6.5g
Fiber ------------------- 3g
Sodium ------------------- 409mg
Potassium ------------------- 142mg

INGREDIENTS

1 1/2 spring onions
250 g potatoes
375 g peas (frozen)
1/2 cup vegetable broth
1 tbsp rapeseed oil
1 tbsp sour cream

 DIRECTIONS

1. Clean the spring onions and cut them into rings.
2. Peel the potatoes and cut them into cubes.
3. Measure 1 cup of peas and set aside.
4. Heat a saucepan over medium heat and add the rapeseed oil.
5. Fry the spring onions in the oil until golden.
6. Add the potatoes and peas to the pot and saute, stirring occasionally.
7. Deglaze the pot with the vegetable broth and cook everything over low heat for about 20 minutes.
8. Puree the soup with an immersion blender until smooth.
9. Stir in the sour cream and season with salt and pepper to taste.
10. Bring the soup to a brief boil then serve.

Meatless Ball Soup

Preparation Time: 10 minutes
Cook Time: 14 minutes

Servings: 4

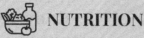 **NUTRITION**

Calories	240	Protein	35g
Carbs	9g	Glycemic Load	5
Sugar	3g		
Fat	10g		

INGREDIENTS

1 lb minced tofu
0.5 lb chopped vegetables
2 cups low-sodium vegetable broth
1 tbsp almond flour
Salt and pepper to taste

DIRECTIONS

1. Mix the tofu, almond flour, salt, and pepper in a bowl.
2. Form the mixture into meatballs.
3. Place the meatballs and chopped vegetables in your Instant Pot.
4. Pour the vegetable broth over the ingredients.
5. Cook on the "Stew" setting for 15 minutes.
6. Allow the pressure to release naturally.

Chicken Zoodle Soup

Preparation Time: 15 minutes
Cook Time: 35 minutes

Servings:2

NUTRITION

Calories -------------------- 250
Carbs -------------------- 5g
Sugar -------------------- 0g
Fat -------------------- 10g
Protein -------------------- 40g
Glycemic Load -------------------- 1

INGREDIENTS

1 lb chopped cooked chicken
1 lb spiralized zucchini
1 cup low-sodium chicken soup
1 cup diced vegetables

DIRECTIONS

In your Instant Pot, mix all the ingredients except the zucchini.
2. Cook on the "Stew" setting for 35 minutes.
3. Allow the pressure to release naturally.
4. Stir in the zucchini and let it heat thoroughly.

Red Lentil Soup

Preparation Time: 10 minutes
Cook Time: 55 minutes

Servings: 8

NUTRITION

Calories -------------------- 284
Total Fat ------------------- 2g
Cholesterol ------------------ 0mg
Sodium ------------------ 419mg
Total Carbohydrates ----------------
--- 47g
Sugar ------------------- 4g
Fiber ------------------- 24g
Protein ------------------- 20g

 DIRECTIONS

1. Heat the oil:Place a large stockpot on medium-high heat and add the extra-virgin olive oil.
2. Saute onion and garlic:Add the chopped onion and minced garlic to the pot and saute until translucent, about 3 minutes.
3. Add celery and carrots:Stir in the chopped celery and diced carrots and continue to saute for 5 minutes.
4. Combine lentils and liquids:Add the red lentils, vegetable broth, water, and bay leaves to the pot. Bring the mixture to a boil.
5. Simmer the soup:Reduce the heat to low and simmer the soup until the lentils are soft and the soup is thick, about 45 minutes.
6. Finish and season:Remove the bay leaves from the soup and stir in the chopped fresh thyme. Season with sea salt and freshly ground black pepper to taste.
7. Serve: Ladle the soup into bowls and serve hot.

INGREDIENTS

1 teaspoon extra-virgin olive oil
1 sweet onion, chopped
1 tablespoon minced garlic
4 celery stalks, with the greens, chopped
3 carrots, peeled and diced
3 cups red lentils, picked over, washed, and drained
4 cups low-sodium vegetable broth
3 cups water
2 bay leaves
2 teaspoons chopped fresh thyme
Sea salt, to taste
Freshly ground black pepper, to taste

Roasted Tomato Bell Pepper Soup

 Preparation Time: 20 minutes
Cook Time: 35minutes

Servings: 6

NUTRITION

Calories -------------------- 188
Total Fat -------------------- 10g
Cholesterol ------------------- 10mg
Sodium ------------------- 826mg
Total Carbohydrates -----------------
--- 21g
Sugar ------------------- 14g
Fiber ------------------- 6g
Protein ------------------- 8g

 INGREDIENTS

2 tablespoons extra-virgin olive oil,
plus more to oil the pan
16 plum tomatoes, cored, halved
4 red bell peppers, seeded, halved
4 celery stalks, coarsely chopped
1 sweet onion, cut into eighths
4 garlic cloves, lightly crushed
Sea salt
Freshly ground black pepper
6 cups low-sodium chicken broth
2 tablespoons chopped fresh basil
2 ounces goat cheese

 DIRECTIONS

1. Preheat the oven to 400°F.
2. Lightly oil a large baking dish
with olive oil.
3. Place the tomatoes cut-side
down in the dish, then scatter the
bell peppers, celery, onion, and
garlic on the tomatoes.
4. Drizzle the vegetables with 2
tablespoons of olive oil and lightly
season with salt and pepper.
5. Roast the vegetables until they
are soft and slightly charred,
about 30 minutes.
6. Remove the vegetables from
the oven and puree them in
batches, with the chicken broth, in
a food processor or blender until
smooth.
7. Transfer the pureed soup to a
medium saucepan over medium-
high heat and bring the soup to a
simmer.
8. Stir in the basil and goat
cheese just before serving.

Lemon-Tarragon Soup

 NUTRITION

Calories -------------------- 136
Carbohydrates -------------------- 3g
Fiber ------------------- 1.1g

 INGREDIENTS

1 tablespoon avocado oil
1/2cup diced onion
3 garlic cloves, crushed
1/4teaspoon plus 1/8 teaspoon sea salt
1/4teaspoon plus 1/8 teaspoon freshly ground black pepper
1(13.5-ounce) can full-fat coconut milk
1 tablespoon freshly squeezed lemon juice
1/2cup raw cashews
1 celery stalk
2 tablespoons chopped fresh tarragon

 DIRECTIONS

1. Saute aromatics:In a medium skillet over medium-high heat, warm the avocado oil. Add the diced onion, crushed garlic, sea salt, and black pepper. Saute for 3 to 5 minutes or until the onion becomes soft and translucent.
2. Blend the ingredients: In a high-speed blender, combine the coconut milk, freshly squeezed lemon juice, raw cashews, celery stalk, and chopped fresh tarragon with the sauteed onion mixture. Blend until smooth.
3. Adjust seasonings:Taste the soup and adjust the seasonings if necessary.
4. Serve:Pour the soup into one large or two small bowls and enjoy immediately. Alternatively, transfer the blended soup to a medium saucepan and warm on low heat for 3 to 5 minutes before serving.

Italian Sausage Soup

 Preparation Time: 10 minutes
Cook Time: 7 minutes

 Servings:6

NUTRITION

Calories -------------------- 280
Fat -------------------- 12.6g
Protein -------------------- 15.4g
Carbohydrates ----------- 24.3g

 ## INGREDIENTS

1 lb ground pork
1 large onion, chopped
2 cups fresh kale, chopped
3/4 lb tiny red new potatoes, cut into pieces
4 cups low-sodium chicken broth
1 teaspoon oregano
2 tablespoons cornstarch
1 (12-ounce) can fat-free evaporated milk
2 cloves garlic, finely diced
1/4teaspoon sea salt
1/4to 1/2 teaspoon crushed red pepper

 ## DIRECTIONS

1. Place a skillet over medium-high heat and cook the ground pork, garlic, and onion until the meat is browned. Drain any excess fat from the pan.

2. Return the meat to the skillet, add the seasonings, and cook for an additional minute.

3. Transfer the meat mixture to your crock pot, then add the potatoes and chicken broth. Cover and cook on low for 6-8 hours or on high for 3-4 hours.

4. In a small bowl, whisk together the cornstarch and evaporated milk until smooth. Add this mixture to the crock pot along with the chopped kale.

5. Cook for about 60 minutes, or until the soup begins to bubble around the edges.

6. Serve topped with crushed red pepper flakes, and enjoy!

Korean Beef Soup

 Preparation Time: 16 minutes
Cook Time: 4 minutes

Servings: 8

NUTRITION

Calories -------------------- 120
Fat ------------------- 4g
Protein ------------------- 18g

 **DIRECTIONS**

1. Set the crock pot to high and add the water.
2. In a mixing bowl, combine the soy sauce, green onions, sesame seeds, oil, sea salt, and black pepper. Divide the mixture evenly between two Ziploc bags.
3. Place the cubed beef in one bag and the diced radish in the other. Let them marinate for 1 hour.
4. Turn the crock pot to low and add the contents of the meat bag. Cook for 1 hour.
5. Add the contents of the radish bag to the crock pot and cook for an additional 3-4 hours.
6. Serve hot and enjoy!

 INGREDIENTS

1 gallon water
1 tablespoon oil
3 tablespoons soy sauce
1 tablespoon toasted sesame seeds
2 cloves garlic, finely diced
1 teaspoon sea salt
1 teaspoon ground black pepper
1 lb beef, cubed
1 Korean white radish, peeled and diced
1 cup green onions, diced

Cream of Broccoli Soup

Preparation Time: 10 minutes
Cook Time:10 minutes

Servings: 4

 NUTRITION

Calories -------------------- 134
Total Fat -------------------- 1.1g
Saturated Fat --------- 0.5g
Monounsaturated Fat --- 0.3g
Polyunsaturated Fat ------ 0.2g
Cholesterol ------------------- 6mg
Sodium ------------------- 160mg
Carbohydrate ----------- 19.8g
Dietary Fiber ------ 2.6g
Sugars -------------------- 1.7g
Starches ------------------- 0.4g
Protein ------------------- 12g

INGREDIENTS

3 tablespoons all-purpose flour
1 2/3 cups homemade chicken broth divided
2 tablespoons fat-free cream cheese
1 10-ounce package frozen chopped broccoli, thawed
1 cup evaporated nonfat milk
1/2 cup skim milk
1 ounce shredded reduced-fat, reduced-sodium, mild white Cheddar cheese
Dash ground black pepper, or to taste
Pinch salt substitute
1 tablespoon chopped fresh parsley, optional for garnish

DIRECTIONS

1. In a small bowl, mix 3 tablespoons of flour with 3 tablespoons of chicken broth until a smooth paste forms.

2. In a large pot, bring the remaining chicken broth to a boil over medium-high heat.

3. Stir in the flour paste, constantly stirring until the soup thickens, about 1 minute. Reduce the heat to medium.

4. Remove 1/4 cup of hot soup from the pot and place it in a bowl. Add the cream cheese and stir until smooth, then pour the mixture back into the pot.

5. Add the broccoli, skim milk, and cheese. Season with a small amount of pepper and salt substitute. Continue stirring and cook until hot and thickened, about 5 minutes.

6. Ladle the soup into small bowls. If desired, sprinkle with fresh parsley for garnish and serve hot.

Chapter :7

SALAD

Carrot Salad

Preparation Time: 10 minutes
Cook Time: 0 minutes

Servings:4

 NUTRITION

Calories	76
Total Fat	3.6g
Saturated Fat	0.5g
Monounsaturated Fat	2.5g
Polyunsaturated Fat	0.4g
Cholesterol	0mg
Sodium	37mg
Carbohydrate	10.9g
Dietary Fiber	3.2g
Sugars	0g
Starches	0g
Protein	1.1g

INGREDIENTS

1 tablespoon extra-virgin olive oil
1 1/2 tablespoons lemon juice
Pinch of salt
1/8 teaspoon freshly ground black pepper
2 cups shredded, peeled carrots

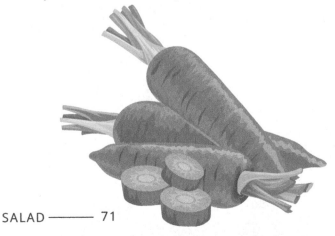

 **DIRECTIONS**

1. In a large bowl, whisk together the olive oil, lemon juice, salt, and pepper.
2. Add the shredded carrots and tos to combine.
3. Serve immediately or cover and refrigerate until ready to use.

Tuna Salad

 Preparation Time: 10 minutes
Cook Time: 0 minutes

Servings: 3

NUTRITION

Calories -------------------- 212
Carbohydrates ----------- 4.8g
Protein -------------------- 14.3g

 **DIRECTIONS**

1. Prepare the dressing by combining olive oil, lime juice, minced garlic, and black pepper.
2. In a salad bowl, mix the tuna, cucumber, tomato, avocado, and celery.
3. Drizzle the salad with the prepared dressing and toss to combine.

 INGREDIENTS

1 (6 oz.) can tuna
1/3 cup fresh cucumber, chopped
1/3 cup fresh tomato, chopped
1/3 cup avocado, chopped
1/3 cup celery, chopped
2 garlic cloves, minced
4 teaspoons olive oil
2 tablespoons lime juice
Pinch of black pepper

Greek Salad

 Preparation Time: 15 minutes
Cook Time:10 minutes

 Servings: 6

NUTRITION

Calories -------------------- 113
Total Fat -------------------- 7.4g
Saturated Fat -------- 3.3g
Monounsaturated Fat ----- 3.1g
Polyunsaturated Fat -------- 0.6g
Cholesterol -------------------- 17mg
Sodium -------------------- 360mg
Carbohydrate ---------- 9.8g
Dietary Fiber ---------- 2.6g
Sugars -------------------- 0.3g
Starches -------------------- 0g
Protein -------------------- 4.7g

 **DIRECTIONS**

1. In a medium bowl, whisk together the olive oil, red wine vinegar, oregano, basil, thyme, and black pepper.

2. In a large bowl, toss the iceberg lettuce, romaine lettuce, cherry tomatoes, cucumber slices, and kalamata olives with enough dressing to coat well.

3. Divide the salad mixture among 6 plates.

4. Top each salad with crumbled feta cheese and a green bell pepper ring.

 **INGREDIENTS**

1 tablespoon olive oil
3 tablespoons red wine vinegar
1 teaspoon dried oregano
1/8 teaspoon dried basil
Pinch of dried thyme
1/4 teaspoon freshly ground black pepper
5 cups iceberg lettuce, torn into bite-size pieces
5 cups romaine lettuce, torn into bite-size pieces
18 cherry tomatoes
1 medium cucumber, peeled, halved, seeded, and sliced
6 kalamata olives
4 ounces feta cheese, crumbled
1 green bell pepper, sliced into 6 rings

Fresh Diced Vegetable Salad

🕐 Preparation Time: 10 minutes
Cook Time: 5 minutes

🍴 Servings: 2

 NUTRITION

Calories	-------------------- 195	Fiber	-------------------- 4.0g
Fat	-------------------- 10.0g	Sugar	-------------------- 3.0g
Protein	-------------------- 17.0g	Sodium	-------------------- 440mg
Carbs	-------------------- 12.0g		

📝 INGREDIENTS

2 small zucchinis, diced
1/2 cucumber, diced
1 red bell pepper, diced
1 green bell pepper, diced
1 yellow bell pepper, diced
1/2 red onion, diced
1 hot house tomato, diced
1 cup cooked chickpeas, rinsed
1/2 cup roughly chopped parsley
1 cup crumbled feta cheese
1 clove garlic, minced
1/2 tablespoon kosher salt (use less if using fine salt)
1 tablespoon freshly ground black pepper
1 tablespoon dried oregano
1/2 cup olive oil
3 tablespoons red wine vinegar

🥗 DIRECTIONS

1. In a large bowl, mix all the diced vegetables, chickpeas, parsley, feta cheese, minced garlic, salt, black pepper, and dried oregano.
2. In a separate smaller bowl, whisk together the olive oil and red wine vinegar to create the dressing.
3. Pour the dressing over the salad and gently toss to coat everything evenly.
4. Serve and enjoy the salad on its own or with a preferred protein.

Mediterranean Bean and Tuna Salad

Preparation Time: 15 minutes
Cook Time: 0 minutes

Servings:4

 NUTRITION

Calories -------------------- 194
Total Fat -------------------- 4.3g
Saturated Fat ------------ 0.5g
Monounsaturated Fat -------- 2.6g
Polyunsaturated Fat ------- 0.7g
Cholesterol ------------------ 14mg
Sodium -------------------- 387mg
Carbohydrate ----------- 20.7g
Dietary Fiber ---------- 5.1g
Sugars -------------------- 2.7g
Starches -------------------- 9.5g
Protein -------------------- 17.4g

 INGREDIENTS

3 small tomatoes, quartered
1/4 cup chopped Vidalia onion or yellow onion
1 scallion, finely chopped
1 (15.5-ounce) can low-sodium cannellini beans, rinsed and drained
1 tablespoon chopped fresh Italian parsley
1 tablespoon olive oil
1 tablespoon lemon juice
1 teaspoon balsamic vinegar
1 teaspoon honey
1 garlic clove, minced
1 (7-ounce) can solid white albacore tuna,packed in water,drained and flaked

 **DIRECTIONS**

1. In a large bowl, combine the tomatoes, onion, scallion, beans, and parsley.
2. In a small bowl, whisk together the olive oil, lemon juice, balsamic vinegar, honey, and garlic.
3. Pour the dressing over the bean mixture and toss to combine.
4. Add the flaked tuna to the salad and toss gently.

Salmon and Quinoa Bowl

DIRECTIONS

1. In a small pot, combine the quinoa and water. Bring to a boil over medium-high heat. Cover, reduce the heat, and simmer for 15 minutes.

2. Preheat the oven to 425°F (220°C). Line a large baking sheet with parchment paper.

3. Place the salmon fillets on one side of the prepared baking sheet. Toss the asparagus with 1 teaspoon of olive oil and arrange on the other side of the baking sheet. Season both the salmon and asparagus with 1/4 teaspoon of salt, 1/4 teaspoon of pepper, and the red pepper flakes. Roast for 12 minutes until browned and cooked through.

4. While the salmon and asparagus are cooking, in a large mixing bowl, gently toss the cooked quinoa, chopped avocado, scallions, cilantro, and oregano. Add the remaining 2 tablespoons of olive oil and the lime juice, and mix well.

5. Break the salmon into pieces, removing the skin and any bones, and chop the asparagus into bite-sized pieces. Fold them into the quinoa mixture.

6. Serve the salmon and quinoa bowl warm or at room temperature.

Preparation Time: 15 minutes
Cook Time: 15 minutes

Servings:4

 NUTRITION

Calories -------------------- 397
Total Fat ------------------- 22g
Protein -------------------- 29g
Carbohydrates ------------ 23g
Sugars -------------------- 3g
Fiber -------------------- 8g
Sodium -------------------- 292mg

 INGREDIENTS

1/2 cup quinoa
1 cup water
4 (4-ounce) salmon fillets
1 pound asparagus, trimmed
1 teaspoon extra-virgin olive oil
1/2 teaspoon salt, divided
1/2 teaspoon freshly ground black pepper, divided
1/4 teaspoon red pepper flakes
1 avocado, chopped
1/4 cup chopped scallions (both white and green parts)
1/4 cup chopped fresh cilantro
1 tablespoon minced fresh oregano
Juice of 1 lime

Strawberry-Arugula Salad

⏰ Preparation Time: 10 minutes
Cook Time: 0 minutes

🍴 Servings: 2

🥗 **NUTRITION**

Calories -------------------- 41
Protein -------------------- 0.2g
Fat -------------------- 0.4g
Carbohydrates ------------ 20g

 INGREDIENTS

1/4 cup fresh parsley leaves, chopped
2 cups arugula
1/2 cup strawberries, quartered
1/4 cup fresh basil leaves
3 tablespoons lemon vinaigrette
1/4 cup red onion, thinly sliced
Thinly sliced almonds (optional) for topping

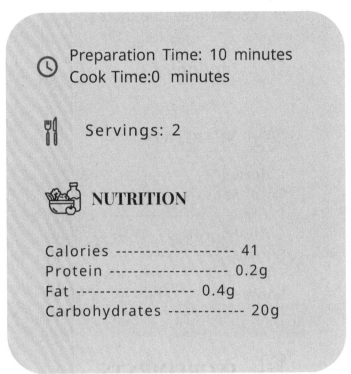

 DIRECTIONS

1. Toss the chopped parsley, arugula, and basil leaves in a salad bowl.
2. Add the lemon vinaigrette, quartered strawberries, and thinly sliced red onion to the salad bowl. Toss again to combine.
3. Season the prepared salad with salt and pepper to taste.
4. Optionally, top the salad with thinly sliced almonds.
5. Serve and enjoy!

Chicken Salad

Preparation Time: 15 minutes
Cook Time:10 minutes

Servings: 2

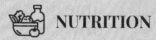 **NUTRITION**

Calories -------------------- 90
Protein ------------------- 12g
Fat ------------------- 7g
Carbohydrates -------------------- 0g

 INGREDIENTS

1/2 (10 ounces) package leafy
lettuce
1 1/2 cups rotisserie chicken
1/3 cup sliced almonds
1 garlic clove, minced
1 carrot, shredded
1/2 cucumber, shredded
2 tablespoons olive oil
1 teaspoon honey 1 1/2 teaspoons
ginger, shredded
1 tablespoon soy sauce
1 tablespoon rice vinegar
1 teaspoon honey

 DIRECTIONS

1. Fry the sliced almonds in a pan until golden brown, then allow
them to cool.
2. In a large mixing bowl, combine the shredded cucumber, shredded
carrot, shredded lettuce, and rotisserie chicken.
3. In a small mixing bowl, mix together the minced garlic, shredded
ginger, honey, soy sauce, and rice vinegar.
4. Pour the soy sauce mixture over the salad and toss to combine.
5. Serve and enjoy!

Orange-Avocado Salad

Preparation Time: 10 minutes
Cook Time: 0 minutes

Servings:2

 NUTRITION

Calories -------------------- 30
Protein -------------------- 2g
Fat -------------------- 2g
Carbohydrates -------------------- 1g

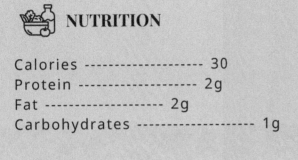 INGREDIENTS

1/2 teaspoon arugula
1 avocado
1 navel orange
1 tablespoon fresh lime juice
1 tablespoon extra-virgin olive oil

 DIRECTIONS

1. In a bowl, mix together the fresh lime juice, arugula, and extra-virgin olive oil.
2. Peel the navel orange and divide it into segments. Add the orange segments to the bowl and toss to coa them with the dressing.
3. Just before serving, dice the avocado and add it to the salad.
4. Toss gently to combine all the ingredients.
5. Serve and enjoy!

Zucchini Salmon Salad

Preparation Time: 10 minutes
Cook Time: 15 minutes

Servings: 2

NUTRITION

Calories -------------------- 109
Fat ------------------- 2g
Protein ------------------- 4g
Carbohydrates ---------- 21g
Fiber ------------------- 6g
Sugar ------------------ 5g
Sodium -------------------- 123mg

DIRECTIONS

1. Wash and peel the zucchini, then cut into thin strips. A spiral cutter works well for this.
2. Lightly fry the zucchini strips in a little olive oil until tender. Allow them to cool and pat dry with kitchen paper. Place the zucchini strips in a salad bowl.
3. Cut the smoked salmon into slices or have it cut at a specialist store.
4. If using basil, wash, drain, and finely chop it. Add the basil and smoked salmon to the zucchini.
5. Add lemon juice, salt, and pepper. Stir the salad well to combine. Adjust seasoning if necessary.
6. Serve and enjoy!

INGREDIENTS

400 g zucchini
100 g smoked salmon
2 tbsp olive oil
2 tbsp lemon juice
Salt and pepper to taste
Fresh basil (optional), finely chopped

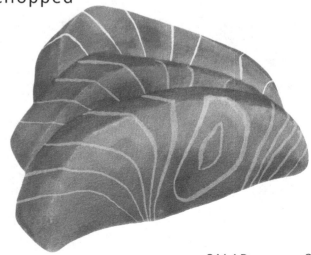

Chapter 8:

DESSERT

Almond Cheesecake Bites

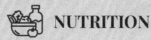

Preparation Time: 5 minutes
Cook Time:0 minutes

Servings: 6

 NUTRITION

Calories -------------------- 68
Protein--------------------- 5g
Fat------------------------- 5g

INGREDIENTS

1/2 cup reduced-fat cream cheese, softened
1/2 cup almonds, ground fine
1/4 cup almond butter
2 drops liquid stevia

 DIRECTIONS

1. In a large bowl, beat together the cream cheese, almond butter, and stevia on high speed until the mixture is smooth and creamy. Cover and chill in the refrigerator for 30 minutes.
2. Once chilled, use your hands to shape the mixture into 12 balls.
3. Place the ground almonds on a shallow plate. Roll each ball in the almonds, ensuring all sides are completely covered.
4. Store the cheesecake bites in an airtight container in the refrigerator.

Almond Coconut Biscotti

 Preparation Time: 5 minutes
Cook Time: 51 minutes

 Servings:6

 NUTRITION

Calories -------------------- 234
Protein -------------------- 5g
Fat -------------------- 18g

INGREDIENTS

1 egg, room temperature
1 egg white, room temperature
1/2 cup margarine, melted
2 1/2 cups flour
1 1/3 cups unsweetened grated coconut
3/4cup sliced almonds
2/3 cup Splenda
2 tsp baking powder
1 tsp vanilla extract
1/2 tsp salt

 **DIRECTIONS**

1. Preheat the oven to 350°F (175°C) Line a baking sheet with parchment paper.
2. In a large bowl, combine the flour, grated coconut, sliced almonds, Splenda, baking powder, and salt.
3. In a separate mixing bowl, beat the egg, egg white, melted margarine and vanilla extract together. Add this wet mixture to the dry ingredients and mix until thoroughly combined.
4. Divide the dough in half. Shape each half into a loaf measuring 8x2 ¾ inches. Place the loaves on the prepared baking sheet, spacing them 3 inches apart.
5. Bake for 25-30 minutes or until the loaves are set and golden brown. Cool on a wire rack for 10 minutes.
6. Using a serrated knife, cut each loaf diagonally into ½-inch slices. Place the slices cut side down back o the baking sheet and bake for anothe 20 minutes, or until firm and nicely browned.
7. Store the biscotti in an airtight container. The serving size is 2 cookies.

Toasted Almond Biscotti

🥣 DIRECTIONS

1. Preheat the oven to 375°F (190°C).
2. In a medium bowl, beat the Splenda and margarine with an electric mixer. Add the egg whites and almond extract and mix well.
3. In a large bowl, combine the flour, baking powder, and salt. Mix in the egg mixture and the chopped almonds.
4. Form the dough into a ball and cut it in half. Roll each half into a 12-inch log, then flatten each log until it is 2 1/2 inches wide. Sprinkle and press 1 tablespoon of sliced almonds lightly into each loaf.
5. Place each loaf on a nonstick baking sheet and bake for 20 minutes, or until the outside of the loaf becomes golden. Remove the loaves to a large cutting board; when cool enough to handle, slice each loaf into 15 3/4-inch-thick slices.
6. Return the sliced biscotti to the baking sheet and bake for 10 minutes. Flip the slices and bake for another 5 to 7 minutes, or until golden.
7. Serve the biscotti warm or store them in an airtight container once they are completely cooled. Note: Putting warm biscotti in a sealed container will affect their crispness and texture.

🕐 Preparation Time: 15 minutes
Cook Time: 0 minutes

🍴 Servings: 6

 NUTRITION

Calories -------------------- 55
Total Fat ------------------ 2.2g
Saturated Fat --------- 0.2g
Monounsaturated Fat ----- 1.3g
Polyunsaturated Fat --------- 0.5g
Cholesterol ------------------- 0mg
Sodium ------------------- 79mg
Carbohydrate -------------------- 7g
Dietary Fiber ----------- 0.6g
Sugars ------------------- 0g
Starches -------------------- 0.1g
Protein ------------------- 2g

📋 INGREDIENTS

1/2 cup Splenda Granular
2 tablespoons light margarine
4 egg whites, lightly beaten
2 teaspoons almond extract
2 cups all-purpose flour
2 teaspoons baking powder
1/4 teaspoon salt
1/4 cup finely chopped toasted almonds
2 tablespoons sliced almonds

Apple Spice Cake

Preparation Time: 15 minutes
Cook Time: 35 minutes

Servings: 8

NUTRITION

Calories -------------------- 201
Fat -------------------- 5.4g
Sodium -------------------- 55.6mg
Carbs -------------------- 34.2g
Fiber -------------------- 3.5g
Sugar -------------------- 21.5g
Protein -------------------- 5.3g

INGREDIENTS

2/3 cup light whipped dessert
1 large apple, cored and finely chopped
1 tablespoon molasses
3 tablespoons vegetable oil
1/4 cup unsweetened applesauce
1/3 cup packed brown sugar
1 (6 oz) carton plain low-fat yogurt
1 egg, beaten
1/8 teaspoon ground cloves
1/4 teaspoon salt
1/2 teaspoon ground ginger
1/2 teaspoon baking soda
1 teaspoon ground cinnamon
1 teaspoon baking powder
1/4 cup flaxseed meal
3/4 cup whole wheat flour
1/4 cup all-purpose flour

DIRECTIONS

1. Preheat the oven to 350 degrees Fahrenheit. Coat a baking pan with cooking spray.
2. In a bowl, combine the whole wheat flour, all-purpose flour, flaxseed meal, 3/4 teaspoon cinnamon, baking powder, baking soda, salt, cloves, and ground ginger.
3. In another bowl, mix together the yogurt, beaten egg, brown sugar, vegetable oil, applesauce, and molasses.
4. Gradually add the egg mixture to the flour mixture, stirring until well combined. Fold in the chopped apple.
5. Spread the batter evenly into the prepared pan.
6. Bake for 35 minutes or until a toothpick inserted into the center comes out clean.
7. Serve warm.

Cranberry-Orange Biscotti

⏰ Preparation Time: 20 minutes
Cook Time:40 minutes

🍴 Servings: 36

🥗 NUTRITION

Calories -------------------- 65
Total Fat ------------------- 2.9g
Saturated Fat -------------- 0.6g
Monounsaturated Fat -- 1.3g
Starches ------------------- 0.1g
Protein -------------------- 1.2g

Polyunsaturated Fat ------ 0.9g
Cholesterol -------------------- 12mg
Sodium -------------------- 49mg
Carbohydrate ----------- 8.3g
Dietary Fiber ------- 0.3g
Sugars -------------------- 2.1g

📋 INGREDIENTS

2 1/4 cups all-purpose flour
1 1/2 teaspoons baking powder
Pinch of salt
1/2 cup margarine
1/4 cup light brown sugar
2 eggs
1 teaspoon pure vanilla extract
2 tablespoons minced orange zest
1/4 cup minced dried cranberries

DIRECTIONS

1. Preheat the oven to 375 degrees F.
2. In a large bowl, mix together the flour, baking powder, and salt.
3. In another bowl, beat the margarine and sugar until creamy, about 2 minutes. Beat in the eggs and vanilla extract. Stir in the flour mixture, orange zest, and dried cranberries.
4. Form the dough into a ball and cut it in half. Roll each half into a 15-inch log, then flatten each log until it is 2 1/2 inches wide. Place each flattened loaf on a nonstick baking sheet and bake for 20 minutes, or until golden.
5. Remove the loaves to a large cutting board; when cool enough to handle, slice each loaf into 18 3/4-inch-thick slices.
6. Return the sliced biscotti to the baking sheet and bake for 10 minutes. Flip the slicesand bake for another 10 minutes, or until the biscotti turn golden.
7. Serve the biscotti warm or store them in an airtight container once they are completely cooled.

Moist and Chewy Peanut Butter Cookies

Preparation Time: 15 minutes
Cook Time:12 minutes

Servings:12

NUTRITION

Calories -------------------- 82
Total Fat ------------------- 3.5g
Saturated Fat ------------ 0.7g
Monounsaturated Fat ------ 1.3g
Polyunsaturated Fat ---- 1.1g
Cholesterol ------------------ 0mg
Sodium -------------------- 83mg
Carbohydrate ------------ 10.7g
Dietary Fiber ----------- 0.8g
Sugars -------------------- 1.6g
Starches -------------------- 0.9g
Protein ------------------- 2.5g

INGREDIENTS

3/4 cup all-purpose flour
1/4 cup whole wheat flour
1 teaspoon baking powder
1 tablespoon orange juice
2 tablespoons water
1 tablespoon unsweetened applesauce
1/2 teaspoon pure vanilla extract
1 egg white
1/4 cup light margarine
2 teaspoons granulated sugar
3 tablespoons reduced-fat creamy peanut butter

DIRECTIONS

1. Combine all ingredients in a large bowl. Cover with plastic wrap and refrigerate for 3 hours.
2. Preheat oven to 350 degrees F.
3. Roll the chilled dough into 12 balls and place on a nonstick baking sheet, spaced at least 2 inches apart. Press each ball down with the tines of a fork facing one direction, then press down again a half-turn around to form a criss-cross pattern.
4. Bake for 12 minutes, or until just crisp around the edges.
5. Cool on a wire rack.

Conclusion

A diabetic diet need not be tasteless. There are many recipes that diabetic patients can make to enjoy healthy and delicious dishes. This book will serve as a guide for those who want to eat well while maintaining healthy blood sugar levels. A diagnosis of diabetes can be overwhelming, but with proper management through diet and lifestyle changes, it is possible to live a healthy and fulfilling life. A diabetes-friendly diet does not mean giving up favorite foods but rather making informed choices and practicing moderation. This cookbook aims to guide you through the initial stages of dietary adjustments, offering practical advice and recipes to help you navigate this journey.

Diabetes is a metabolic disorder that occurs when the pancreas is unable to produce sufficient insulin. Insulin is needed for blood glucose (sugar) to enter cells and be used as fuel. When insulin is insufficient, blood glucose remains in the bloodstream, depriving the body of its main source of energy. In response, the body turns to stored sugar in the form of glycogen and fat within cells.

A healthy diet and regular exercise are crucial for managing diabetes. When the body lacks enough insulin, glucose builds up in the blood, damaging blood vessels and nerves, which can lead to serious complications such as blindness, kidney damage, and heart disease. Monitoring carbohydrate intake and blood glucose levels is essential for diabetic patients.

This book provides some of the best diabetic diet recipes, which help in reducing carbohydrate intake and losing weight. These recipes are also low in sodium and saturated fats. Diabetic individuals can try these recipes to reduce the risk of complications and live a healthy life. The recipes are easy to follow and include complete nutritional information and dietary guidelines, allowing individuals with diabetes to enjoy delicious meals while maintaining their health.

Prevention of diabetes complications comes from eating healthy food and exercising regularly. Many diabetics have successfully controlled their condition through proper diet and exercise. Knowing what you can eat depending on your type of diabetes is essential for staying on track with your health. Proper diet and exercise are the best ways to control type 2 diabetes. Understanding more about diabetes and its management is crucial.

People with type 1 diabetes must take insulin shots to control their diabetes. Those with type 2 diabetes can often control their condition with a balanced diet and frequent physical activity, but they may also need glucose-lowering drugs, which can be taken as tablets or injections.

To manage diabetes effectively, it is important to avoid a diet high in starches, as they tend to raise blood glucose levels. Too many carbohydrates can lead to insulin sensitivity and pancreatic fatigue, as well as weight gain with associated risk factors for cardiovascular disease and hypertension. Lowering sugar intake decreases the body's need for insulin and increases fat burning. When your body is low on sugars, it will burn fat for energy, leading to weight loss.

In conclusion, this cookbook is designed to help you maintain good health and enjoy your meals despite a diabetes diagnosis. By following the guidance and recipes provided, you can control your diabetes and lead a healthier, more fulfilling life.

Thank You !

Dear Customer,
We would love to hear your thoughts and suggestions for the author of this book. Please feel free to share your feedback. Additionally, by scanning the QR code, you can access more recipe tutorials and even download a free collection of 2,000 recipes.
Thank you for your support!

https://forms.gle/2RDDh5SnhWQwTLuP7

Author's email: laihongchun70@gmail.com

wish you a happy life!

Made in the USA
Coppell, TX
14 October 2024

38652166R10057